The Key to Goa and Indian Ocean Islands

REG BUTLER

In Association with

THOMSON HOLIDAYS

1995/96

SETTLE PRESS

Text © 1994 Reg Butler

First published by Settle Press
10 Boyne Terrace Mews
London W11 3LR

ISBN (Paperback) 1 872876 33 1
ISBN (Hardback) 1 872876 34 X

Printed by Villiers Publications
19 Sylvan Avenue
London N3 2LE
Maps by Mary Butler

Foreword

As Britain's leading holiday company operating to Goa and other beach destinations of the Indian Ocean, Thomson are happy to be associated with Reg Butler's latest guide-book to the region.

The author has travelled annually for around two dozen years throughout India and other areas, and is well qualified to write about the history, culture and cuisine of these fascinating lands.

Whichever destination you have chosen for your holiday, we feel this pocket book can act as a quick reference guide to the great sightseeing potential beyond the beaches. In writing the book, the author has also worked closely with our own locally-based staff and agents who have year-round contact with holidaymakers' travel interests.

Prices are always a problem during a time of variable inflation and exchange rates. Inevitably there will be some local changes since this edition was printed. However, the prices mentioned should still give a reasonable indication of the average level of expenses to expect.

THOMSON HOLIDAYS

Contents

Chapter One

Explore the Indian Ocean

The third largest ocean after the Pacific and Atlantic, the Indian Ocean covers about one-fifth of the world's water surface.

It is eight times the size of USA, stretching from the Red Sea and Persian Gulf to the borders of Indonesia; along the entire east coast of Africa to the longitude of the Cape of Good Hope; and past the west coast of Australia to Antarctica.

In the tropical zones the water temperature stays generally above an idyllic 80^0 F. This constant temperature is perfect for the off-shore growth of coral reefs. In turn, the coral attracts shoals of variegated tropical fish, while providing sheltered lagoons between the reef and the sandy shorelines.

All these conditions are ideal for modern holiday-makers who dream of warm sunshine, uncrowded beaches, choice of watersports – including snorkelling among the fish – and a hotel setting amid rustling palm trees.

In Goa and Sri Lanka, the long beaches are far removed from industry and big cities. Visitors can enjoy the crystal-clear waters, while having rich sightseeing within easy reach. It's certainly worth tearing oneself away from the golden sands, to savour the cultures of India and old-time Ceylon.

Most of the widely scattered tropical islands of the Indian Ocean were virtually uninhabited until 500 years ago – mainly due to their remote locations, far removed from historic trading routes. Only a few Arab sailors, and then the Portuguese and the Dutch, knew first-hand of the existence of the Maldive Islands, Seychelles and Mauritius.

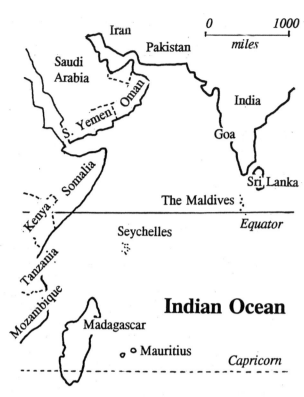

During the age of colonialism, Mauritius and the Seychelles Islands were developed with sugar, spice and coconut plantations, worked initially by African slaves, and later by Indian contract labour. Hence came a rich medley of the cultures of Africa, Asia and Europe. It all adds to the exotic atmosphere of these dreamy islands in the sun.

In contrast to medieval times, when trading dhows hugged the shorelines of Africa and Asia, the Indian Ocean today is a major transportation highway for oil tankers from the Middle East to Europe and the Americas. Factory ships exploit the ocean mainly for shrimp and tuna.

Otherwise the seas remain as empty as ever. It's the age of air transport which has opened these tropical paradise destinations to holidaymakers and honeymooners in search of somewhere 'different'. One can explore and enjoy the Robinson Crusoe scenery in a setting of total comfort.

Chapter Two

Planning to go

2.1 Which season?

Whichever month you choose for Indian Ocean destinations, there'll be guaranteed warm sun. The seasons are mainly determined by the monsoon wind system. North of the equator, northeast winds blow from October until April; from May until October, the winds come from south and west.

Thus, Goa has three seasons: winter, summer and monsoon. The best holiday months are November to March, bone dry and comfortably warm. April until mid-June becomes extremely hot. Then the monsoon takes over with a total 88" of rain until it dries up in October.

In Sri Lanka the pattern is somewhat different, with rains peaking in April-June and in October-November. South of the equator, the drier and cooler months for Seychelles and Mauritius are from May to September. Rains tend to be brief but heavy, cooling down the air and followed by renewed sunbathing weather. See the next page for the average statistics – though monthly variations are always possible.

2.2 Visa regulations

UK, EC, Commonwealth or US citizens do not need visas for Sri Lanka, Seychelles or Mauritius.

But everyone needs a visa for India, obtainable from High Commission of India, India House, Aldwych, London WC2B 4NA. Tel: 0171-836-8484; or at 82-86 New Street, Birmingham B2 4BA Tel: 0121-643-0829.

2.3 What weather to expect:

Max — Average maximum temperatures — °F. Rain — Monthly rainfall in inches.

	Jan	Feb	Mar	Apr	May	Jun	Jul	Aug	Sep	Oct	Nov	Dec	Annual rainfall
GOA													
Max	89	90	90	91	91	87	84	84	85	88	91	91	
Rain	0.1	0.0	0.2	0.4	0.7	22.8	35.1	13.4	10.9	4.8	0.8	1.5	90.7"
DELHI													
Max	70	75	86	97	106	104	95	93	93	95	84	73	
Rain	1.0	0.9	0.7	0.3	0.3	2.6	8.3	6.8	5.9	1.2	0.0	0.2	28.2"
MAURITIUS													
Max (East)	84	84	84	82	79	77	75	75	77	79	82	84	
Max (North)	88	88	88	86	84	81	79	79	81	82	86	88	
Rain (East)	4.5	10.1	9.4	7.2	2.5	1.8	2.3	1.6	2.1	1.4	1.9	5.6	50.4"
Rain (North)	3.6	6.8	4.6	5.6	1.8	1.7	1.3	1.5	1.7	0.7	1.3	3.9	34.5"
SRI LANKA													
Max	86	87	88	88	87	85	85	85	85	85	85	85	
Rain	3.5	2.5	6.0	9.0	14.5	9.0	5.5	4.5	6.5	13.5	12.5	6.0	93.0"
SEYCHELLES													
Max	86	87	88	88	87	84	82	83	84	85	86	86	
Rain	15.4	11.8	7.1	7.6	4.0	2.0	2.5	4.3	4.9	8.7	9.0	12.0	89.4"

2.4 What to pack, and what to wear

Pack light cotton dresses of the drip-dry wash-and-wear variety, and a lightweight suit for up-market evening dining. A wide brimmed beach hat and sun glasses are recommended, and comfortable shoes or sandals. Bring plastic shoes as protection from sharp coral if you're keen on snorkelling or under-water sports. Visitors should be suitably clad when entering temples and shrines.

Hotels provide basic equipment for the usual holiday sports. But dedicated tennis players, for instance, should bring their favourite tennis racket and footwear.

2.5 Health care

There is no *obligation* to produce vaccination certificates when arriving direct from Europe or North America. But some jabs are recommended, and vaccination records should be checked.

Ask your own doctor's advice at least six weeks before departure. Some medical people lean heavily towards ultra-caution, and recommend the full works. Others suggest that some jabs are not essential if you are taking normal care of yourself, and not visiting any outlandish areas.

For further health advice contact the Hospital for Tropical Diseases Healthline on 0839 337 722. Code number is 55. A phone charge is made of 36p a minute in off-peak hours; otherwise 49p a minute.

Mosquitoes

Quite apart from the dreaded female *anopheles* mosquitoes who get the blame for malaria, have your defences ready against all the other varieties of biting insects. Mosquitoes and sand flies bite especially at dusk when hungry for supper. They are very partial to holidaymakers. Be frugal with perfumes and aftershaves, as these seem to attract them. Insect repellents are sold at chemists and in hotel-resort shops.

An excellent mosquito deterrent is (believe-it-or-not) Avon's 'Skin-so-soft' bath oil spray. It's highly effective. Even sand-flies will keep their distance.

COASTAL GOA

Chapter Three

Goa – India's historic gateway

3.1 Go away to Golden Goa

250 miles south of Bombay, as the charter aircraft flies down the west coast of India, long stretches of golden beach are backed by a lush green country-side.

Occupied by the Portuguese in 1510, the city of Old Goa became the capital of all Portuguese territories in India, and later the administration and religious centre for Portugal's entire empire in the East. The broad estuaries and natural harbours made Goa an ideal base.

For a hundred years the Portuguese kept their trading monopoly in India until the Dutch and then the English established settlements in other areas of the sub-continent. Bypassed for the next few centuries, Goa slumbered in a tranquil backwater until Portugal's 450 years of colonial rule ended in 1961.

The 65 miles of Goan coastline were 'discovered' by the hippies of the 1960's. Attracted by the golden beaches of superb quality, the drop-outs of 30 years ago flocked to this idyllic winter paradise where fish, rice and alcohol were cheap, and a palm-thatched hut could be rented for peanuts.

Following the hippy pioneers, developers built resort hotels that catered for much wealthier visi-tors. Finally the charter flights arrived, to reinstate Goa as an international gateway into the Indian sub-continent.

The way is now open for holiday visitors to combine the pleasures of a tropical beach with the chance of seeing some of the great sightseeing highlights of India.

In contrast to the famous tourist cities and teeming populations elsewhere in India, the largest town and capital of Goa is Panaji with 60,000 people. Most of the remaining 1.2 million inhabitants live in villages. Many of their houses are built of red laterite stone or brick, with several rooms and a verandah. It could be southern Portugal, transplanted among the coconut groves and banyan trees.

Wherever you stay at the developing beach resorts, this life of rural India is only a short walk away. A drive through the evergreen countryside is beautiful everywhere.

All along the coast is a lush belt of coconut groves, with tranquil villages in the shade. Bullock carts take produce to market, while cattle wander in leisured style across the road, heedless of scooters.

The inland hills are a beautiful feature of Goa. Winding country roads pass terraced fields and a myriad fruit trees. Here is the land of cashew nuts, Goa's largest export crop.

A favourite tourist excursion is to a model fruit and spice farm, to watch the harvesting of coconuts, and inspect the plants and trees which produce the ingredients of India's famous curries and chutneys. Most visitors go home with low-cost packets of spices and cashew nuts.

Tropical fruits are part of the holiday. Stubby little bananas have a delicious sweet flavour, far tastier than Britain's imported bananas which are picked green for transport, and ripened artificially. Likewise the local pineapples are sweet and juicy, and served in fat slices.

The best eating in Goa is seafood, cooked in a variety of styles. Along the beaches, shack restaurants serve lobster, tiger prawns, squid, oysters, mussels, crabs, shark mullet, pomfret, grouper and mackerel at less than one-third the cost in hotels and more formal restaurants.

There's no such thing as a crowded beach. The sands are powder-fine, often several hundred yards deep from the shoreline to the palm trees. Colva Beach is the longest on India's west coast.

Very little is left of the hippy scene of 30 years ago, though a few veterans base themselves at

Anjuna Beach, where an ultra-simple room costs only £2 or £3 a night.

The beach resorts are low profile. As a later starter in holiday business, the Goan authorities want to avoid the shoe-box architecture of Mediterranean resorts.

Instead, holiday bungalows and villas are set amid gardens and palm trees, with social life revolving around the pool.

Service standards are high, partly because Goans have long been recruited as staff aboard the world's great cruise liners. Experienced stewards, bartenders and musicians have come ashore and by example are training the younger generation.

Nobody goes to Goa for the nightlife, but beach barbecues and folk entertainment add pleasure to the evenings. Goan music and dancing is a rich cultural mixture of Hindu and Portuguese.

The most favoured musical instrument is the guitar. Popular tunes are sung either in Portuguese or in the Goan mother tongue of Konkani. Many dances and costumes have come virtually unaltered from Portugal.

The Portuguese heritage is seen especially in the religion. At Christmas there are serenades of guitars, mandolins and violins, with the singing of popular carols and the Portuguese love songs called fados. Nearly 40% of the population are Catholics.

Certainly Goa has a character quite distinct from the rest of India. Skirts far outnumber saris and people display an easy going tropical indulgence and civility which you will find hard to beat. Markets are lively colourful affairs and siesta is observed during the hot afternoons.

Although beaches are the focus of a Goan holiday, there is good sightseeing potential within an easy drive.

The great churches of Old Goa are World Heritage Monuments and the scene of Catholic pilgrimage. Only a short distance away are equally interesting Hindu temples which likewise are pilgrim sites.

Above all, there is constant pleasure from that beautiful green countryside.

3.2 Arrival & orientation

Coming in from the north, the aircraft offers a good view of Goa's north coast beaches. First comes the estuary of the River Mandovi – the boundary between the districts of North and South Goa – immediately followed by the much broader Mormugao Bay, which is fed by the River Zuari. Then you see the major cargo terminal of Mormugao itself, which handles Goa's iron ore exports.

The aircraft circles south of Vasco da Gama, which takes its name from the Portuguese explorer; and then flies over Bogmalo Beach for the landing.

Goa's airport has a vintage Portuguese appearance. A poster may still proclaim 1991 as the Year of Indian Tourism, and a welcoming sign in mid-March can wish everyone a Merry Christmas and Happy New Year.

Standing half an hour for immigration rituals, visitors soon get the message that the pace of life is rather more sedate than elsewhere.

Customs clearance is simple. You are expected to declare the more costly electronic and photographic items, and must pay duty if they are not re-exported when you depart. A faded notice says that five rolls of camera film are the limit for what may be brought in. But there are no searching questions on this point.

Outside the terminal, the travel agency reps and tour buses await. It's a 45-minute journey to Panaji – an essential staging-point for people staying at any of the north beaches. For the south beaches, transfer time is a maximum of 75 minutes. Wherever you're staying, the gorgeous scenery en route is already part of the holiday experience.

3.3 At your service

Money: Subject to fluctuation, the exchange rate of the Indian rupee is around 50 Rs to the pound, or 33 Rs to the US dollar. Currency and travellers cheques are readily exchanged at about the same rate in banks or hotels.

Some banks can give cash against Visa or Access/Mastercard. Passports are required for exchange transactions. Ensure that you are given a receipt, which is required for converting back any remaining rupees on departure.

Transport: Goa now has a reasonable highway system, though local driving techniques may seem hair-raising. Goan road-users often combine Latin panache with a Hindu fatalism that gives them sublime confidence that there'll be nothing coming the other way if they overtake on a bend.

A high proportion of the local male population rides around on scooters and motor-bikes, and even a minority of the women and girls, but hardly anyone wears a helmet. Along tarred roads there is room for about 1½ vehicles, with dirt shoulders on either side. Whoever is chicken can make a last-second swerve into the dust. Wobbling bicycles and aimless animals are an additional hazard.

The message is that motor-bike or car hire is not recommended. However, if you are determined on vehicle rental, come equipped with an International Driving Licence, as the regular licence is not recognised in India. If stopped by a policeman, an on-the-spot fine is levied on anyone without a proper International Licence.

If caught, haggle! The fine can come tumbling down if you protest that you are carrying very little cash. Having negotiated your fine, it's unlikely that any receipt will be given. It all helps policemen to top up their low salaries.

Travelling by local bus is another non-tempting experience. Buses are tightly packed, run to erratic timetables and are liable to delays and breakdowns. However, they are extremely cheap.

There are also more comfortable long-distance inter-State services that are described as Luxury or Air-Conditioned. For the distances involved they are very economical. To Bombay, for instance, the 16-hour 370-mile journey costs under £5.

For local trips, taxis are the answer; or car-rental with driver, which is virtually the same thing.

The best bet in Goa are the white tourist vehicles that stand outside hotels. At many cab-ranks, a display board states the cost to sundry destinations.

Cheap returns

It's usual to arrange a set fee for a return journey, plus 10 to 20 rupees per hour waiting time. In fact the return journey normally costs little more than single.

From Majorda Beach, for instance, typical prices are £2 to Colva one-way, £2.40 return; Panaji £6.40 one-way, £6.60 return; plus waiting charges 40p an hour.

Alternatively you can agree on paying per kilometre and for waiting time. Official tariffs are set, but few vehicles have taximeters. Start off on a proper footing with the driver by writing down the kilometre level when the trip begins, and likewise noting the waiting time at each halt. It saves unhappy arguments when the reckoning comes, and is fairer all round.

Most of the drivers are helpful and courteous, and are familiar with the highlights of tourism. But they are not trained guides.

If you want an informed commentary and a well-planned itinerary, take the travel-agency sightseeing tours by coach or minibus. These often include some entertainment in the programme.

In cities like Panaji – and in the other cities of India – there are regular yellow-top taxis (usually vintage Indian-made Ambassador cars that are old-time Morris Oxford design). If their meter still works, make sure it is turned on.

Owing to inflation, fares do not always conform to readings on the meter. To avoid confusion, ask to see the latest fare chart, and pay accordingly.

There are also auto rickshaws, which are fun and very cheap for short rides. Even cheaper for the ultra-brave are motor-cycle 'taxis' for one passenger only, riding pillion. Not recommended.

For railway buffs, Goa was formerly served only by one line from Bombay to Margao and Vasco da Gama – a 24-hour ordeal.

However, a new rail link called Konkan Railway starts operating during 1995, taking only 8 hours for the same journey.

By air, Bombay is 60 minutes away; Delhi 2½ hours.

3.4 Cultural background

Goa offers a unique cultural mixture of India and Portugal, Hindu and Catholic. Religions co-exist amicably in Goa, which has never had inter-communal violence.

Religious festivals come with great frequency, and are usually celebrated by all the communities. Hindus keep Christmas and enjoy Carnival; Catholics take time off for Shigmo, the Hindu springtime counterpart of Carnival. It's worth making local enquiry about any festivities scheduled during your stay, to enjoy one of these colourful events.

Around 38% of the population are devout Catholics. Goan women wear white or black lace mantillas to Mass, while the Catholic religion is interwoven with the caste system (at least so far as marriage eligibility is concerned). Catholic processions are lively with fire-crackers in the church precincts.

The Catholic creed was established by the Franciscans who arrived in 1517. But the greatest religious fervour came from the Jesuits in mid-16th century, under the inspired leadership of St Francis Xavier who spread his missionary work throughout Asia. Besides their missionary work, the Jesuits also opened schools, founded a hospital and established a printing press.

Possibly that explains the higher literacy level of the Goan people, who are very successful in computer industries, politics, medicine and other professions. The only Indian member of the British parliament is of Goan origin.

Many Goans work in the Gulf, earning good money which they remit back home – often returning to start their own successful businesses, based on experience acquired abroad.

After 450 years of Portuguese influence, Goans talk with Latin gesticulations, have a cheerful and optimistic character, and enjoy an afternoon siesta. The parish schools conducted classes in singing, piano and violin playing, which is reflected today in Goan musical skills.

Many folk-tunes come direct from Portugal. In music, dance and costume there is a marriage of cultures, which also appears in the local cuisine.

3.5 Beach-hopping in south Goa

Goa's tourist industry is built on sand, though the physical accommodation is set well back from the shoreline (no building within 200 metres of the High Tide Line), with strict height restrictions within a 500-metre zone. Foreshore developments have been rigidly controlled in this way since 1991, to preserve the natural look that is one of Goa's greatest shoreline assets.

Only two other States in India regulate tourism in this environmentally friendly way. There is no threat that Goa will become a Spanish-style Costa lined with high-rise concrete.

Wherever you're staying, it's easy to go beach-hopping by scooter or taxi. Organised tours combine a selection of beaches with other sightseeing. Roads go north-south, parallel to the coastline through miles of lush coconut plantations. Minor side-roads turn down to the beaches that are strung like a golden necklace along the entire coast.

Scattered amid the palm groves are the landowners' spacious bungalows, well shaded and traditional in style except for satellite dishes. Notice the stone benches on every verandah, where family and friends exchange gossip.

Colva Beach is the second longest in India, outstripped only by Marina Beach at Madras on the east coast. Four miles from Margao, Colva has adequate shopping, refreshment and changing facilities for day-trip visitors. Everyone can have an acre of space, along a beach that's two hundred yards wide from the ocean to the shoreline palm trees. The sea is warm as new milk.

Facing the village centre of Colva, fishing boats are anchored just offshore, and outriggers are hauled up on the beach. Fishermen spread out their catch to dry in the wind. If you're fond of seafood, the aroma is heavenly.

Otherwise you can choose from literally miles of pristine sand – south to the more secluded beaches of **Benaulim**, **Cavelossim** and **Mabor**; or north towards **Betalbatim** and **Majorda**. They are all totally unspoilt, and offer a scattered range of accommodation, from resort hotels to tourist bunga-lows. A few beach bars and seafood restaurants cater to western tastes. Evening time is great for a stroll, especially with a refreshing sea breeze to help you cool down from the midday heat.

Going north past Majorda, there's another long stretch of beaches – **Cansaulim** and **Velsao** – and thence round to **Bogmalo**, the closest to the airport, only three miles away. Part of that beach is well manicured for guests of the 7-storey Oberoi Hotel – one of the few beachfront properties, built before the stricter building regulations were applied.

Nestling between the Arabian Sea and the Zuari River, **Vasco da Gama** is Goa's most cosmopolitan town. Known locally just as Vasco, it is well laid out in comparison to other Goan towns. It is equi-distant from Dabolim airport and the port of Mormugao which is one of India's major natural harbours, handling very large exports of iron ore.

Vasco is a showcase for wood carvings and handicrafts, handled by several shops near the northern end of Swatantra Path. However, there's not much else to interest keen shoppers. A mile from Vasco is **Baina Beach**, half of which is reasonable, while the other half is rather seedy due to its proximity to a notorious red light area that serves Mormugao.

Across the wide Mormugao Bay a number of delightful small coves are spaced along the fore-shore of the Zuari estuary. Typical of several pleasant holiday beaches is **Dona Paula**, which offers facilities for water scootering. A dozen outrigger fishing boats are pulled up on the sands. Further round the bay, pleasure boats and fore-shores are dedicated to holiday use. All these beaches are within very easy reach of Panaji.

Around the headland into Aguada Bay, **Miramar Beach** stretches along a river promenade into Panaji itself. It's a remarkably good beach, with very wide, golden sand. Here is the setting for a Food and Cultural Festival held annually in the third week of November, and also for Carnival in mid-February. In late March the Shigmo festival heralds the coming of Spring.

3.6 Beach-hopping in north Goa

The Mandovi River marks the boundary between south and north Goa, with the bridges at Panaji providing the principal highway link.

Dominating the northern tip of the estuary is Fort Aguada, which looks out to sea and across to Miramar Beach and Panaji. The huge Portuguese fortress, built square and formidable, is now used as a prison.

Aguada means 'watering place'. In Aguada Bay below the Fort, Portuguese ships traditionally took on their supplies of fresh water for the long voyage home. Today, the watering place is infinitely peaceful, with just a few water buffaloes and some fishing vessels around the landing-stage.

Along the road to the lighthouse beside the prison-fortress, one gets a fine panorama of the ruler-straight beach that stretches north. It goes from Fort Aguada Beach Resort through **Sinquerim Beach** and **Candolim Beach** to **Calangute** and thence to the estuary of the next major river at **Vagator**. The beaches are deep soft sand all the way.

Parallel to the coast, the highway is being ribbon developed with spacious houses in large gardens. Some are used as guest houses. A number of Tibetan and Kashmiri establishments display their handicrafts.

Blocks of the red laterite stone, quarried from local hillsides, are piled ready at building sites. There are even landscape developers at work among the new shop complexes, studios and apartments.

You can see all the growth stages of this new industry of catering for visitors.

First a shack is established on a suitable patch of land. With a roof of thatch or a sheet of corrugated iron, and matting supported by poles for the walls, a man is in business: a refreshment stand, fast Indian food, a bar, a grocery kiosk or a souvenir stall.

Later the walls are made more permanent with laterite building blocks. Then comes painting and decorating, and tiling of the roof, until it all looks quite pristine in contrast to the original shack.

Calangute is the main focus of all this activity, and rates as Goa's most developed beach resort, with easy access to Mapusa and Panaji. This is one of the original hippy beaches, but it's now well served with a full range of hotels, guest houses, restaurants and tourist shops. There are rooms to let, cycles for hire and tourist taxis.

However, the village character is still preserved around Calangute Market, where farmers park their bullock carts in the shade of coconut palms. Just opposite the market is a brightly-coloured Hindu temple.

Baga Beach lies two miles north: a former fishing village, somewhat quieter than Calangute. The two resorts are virtually merging into one, as space is filled with more hotel developments.

The road between Calangute and Anjuna offers gorgeous scenery with green hillsides, fields, coconut palms and plentiful birdlife. White and black goats browse across the harvested fields like gleaners at work.

Anjuna Beach was known as the hippies' heaven, but relatively few aging survivors remain, renting a room or a house for the winter. The beach is set in a series of little coves overlooked by purple cliffs. On Wednesdays a general flea market is held, where people from miles around bring their handicraft products. The few designer hippies are greatly outnumbered by the Kashmiris and the Tibetans.

Vagator and **Small Vagator** are within walking distance of Anjuna. Vagator is a picturesque beach often used as a locale for film shooting. Overlooking the beach is Chapora Fort, on the crest of a headland that commands entry into Chapora River.

Both at Anjuna and Vagator are faded notices that remind today's visitors of the area's former notoriety in the Indian press. The wording is still readable: "Nudism is Prohibited"; or "Don't dabble in drugs. It is a social crime, punishable with ten to thirty years imprisonment."

A beachside shack restaurant offers very basic furnished rooms at £3 a night, with a notice at the entrance: "Beware of touts and drug dabblers."

3.7 Shopping
Market centres

Regular shop hours are Mon-Fri 9-13 and 16-20 hrs, while street markets are more flexible. Friday is the most popular shopping day for local people. Panaji is the principal shopping centre, but the colourful traditional markets at Margao and Mapusa are much more fun, with something different again at Anjuna Beach.

Margao, twenty miles from Panaji, is the congested market centre and administrative capital for south Goa. With major bus and rail terminals, it's the thriving hub of trading and business. The city boasts fine parks and gardens, and imposing Portuguese-built mansions and contemporary buildings.

There are four market places in central Margao: municipal market, fish market, vegetable market and new market. The new market is simply an old market which moved closer into town. The vegetable market is also known as Modki Bazaar, where pots and earthenware are sold.

An indoor market is located near the garden square. It's worth visiting for the interesting sights and smells, thanks to a good range of spices, nuts and leather sandals. Regular shops sell handicrafts, clothes and giftware. Photo stores can develop and print your films at around 200 Rs for 24 prints.

Mapusa is north Goa's principal crossroads and market centre with daily activity that peaks on Friday into a big tourist attraction. It's a good place to buy local crafts and souvenirs, and enjoy the hustle and bustle. Gold and silver jewellery is sold here; and the drums called tabla; spices; readymade garments; nuts; liquors.

Peasant farmers display their produce while sitting, squatting or lying on the ground. Fruit is neatly arranged in pyramids. There are grapes on sale, garlands and garlic. Overall is a tantalising medley of different smells: some good, some bad. Fresh flowers and dried fish are displayed alongside one another, mingling their fragrance.

Most colourful are little sacks of spices; and onions with bright purple skins. Betel leaves are counted out for the making of 'pan'. The more daring visitors may want to sample the range of sweets on display, mostly looking home-made. Some are lightly covered in a thin silver foil which is edible.

Historically, Mapusa's Friday market even acted as an informal marriage market where families could look out for prospective marriage partners for their sons or daughters.

Anjuna Beach features a Wednesday handicrafts market popularised by the hippies. But today the selling is done mainly by the Kashmiris who believe in hard-sell of their shawls, carpets and woodcarvings. In strong contrast are the Tibetan traders who display their wares in much more artistic fashion.

However, some flower-power hippies still gather to sell handmade clothing, bags, rugs and jewellery. You can have your ears pierced and your hair cut. It's a fascinating place for people watching, against the background of a most picturesque beach where you can relax or swim after exploring the market.

What to buy

During a holiday in India, you will almost certainly be tempted to buy souvenirs, and possibly more expensive items such as jewellery and furniture.

There is wide choice of local handicrafts made from wood, brass and marble. Beautiful fabrics are made into all kinds of clothing, and there are good bargains in casual wear.

Indian jewellers are highly skilled in silver filigree and heavy gold work.

State-run emporia with fixed prices, or small shops and bazaars where you can barter, are preferable to street pedlars who usually ask at least three times the realistic price.

Beware of being overcharged at tourist shops, and be ready to haggle. 'Walking away tactics' are usually effective in bringing down the price, especially if you start moving towards a neighbouring shop that sells similar products.

Be careful about costly antiques which may not be authentic. Production of antiques is a flourishing cottage industry.

If a shop undertakes to ship bulkier purchases such as rugs, carpets or furniture, the goods will always take far longer to arrive than is promised. You may have to pay duty and VAT when the package arrives. If you anticipate buying costly items, it's worth checking on the levels of import duty payable before leaving the UK.

Jewellery – Hotel shops are the safest place to buy big items. The price may be slightly higher, but jewellers will give a certificate of authenticity.

Fabrics – The bazaars have cheaper prices, but some of the more special weaves are found in the shops.

Saris – Vary in length throughout the country, so check the local length before you have it made up. When fabric is cut from a long continuous piece, it is sold by the metre length, but the width is still described in inches.

Silk – The average price of raw silk is just over £3 per metre. If you are having clothing tailor-made, don't pay until you are satisfied with the product.

T-shirts – Ideal gifts, costing only about £1 each. Available from market and beach vendors, but haggle!

Pottery – Terracotta pots and artefacts are priced from 10 to 350 Rs from any handicraft store. For more artistic pieces, it is worth visiting Kamarkhazana, near Mapusa, where individual designer items are available.

Decorated boxes – Made from papier-mâché, they come in all shapes and sizes, beautifully decorated.

Leather bags – Excellent quality and unique designs. The best are in the hotel shops.

Carpet & rugs – Prices vary according to the material. Silk carpets are the most expensive. The number of knots and the age of the carpet will also determine the price. Again, the best qualities are usually in the hotel shops.

Cashmere – Prices are about one-third those in the UK.

Spices – Ideal for trying out your favourite curries back home. A complete range is available from the markets at Margao and Mapusa; or in neat packages from the model Spice Farm at Khandepar in Ponda District. Consider this basic shopping list of ten best buys:

Black pepper. Red chillies, ground up and stronger than those one buys in UK. Coriander, ground up. Saffron. Cloves. Cinnamon powder and cinammon sticks. Jeera, normally called cummin. Grated coconut, sun-dried so that it keeps well. Tamarind, to give a sour taste to a dish.

Cashew Nuts – 200-gramme packets make ideal small gifts. Prices depend on the quality. Broken nuts, generally used for cake-making, are the cheapest. Otherwise, cashew nuts are graded according to size - larger ones cost more – but the flavour is just the same. Prices average around £4 a kilo. In Panaji, at least a dozen shops are clustered together, all selling cashew nuts only, in every grade and packet size. Market ladies sell village cashews at three nuts for one rupee.

Wine & feni – Very few people leave Goa without a bottle or two, costing a pound or less, or a little more for whiskies with ambitious brand-names. Port wine is priced from 20 Rs a bottle. The best selections are at bottle stores in towns such as Margao and Panaji.

3.8 Sport, entertainment and nightlife

Sport and leisure facilities are mostly limited to what is offered by the hotels: the usual range of windsurfing, sailing, waterskiing and snorkelling. There are virtually no independent watersport centres on the beaches, nor public tennis courts or golf clubs.

Among the spectator sports, an essential part of many village festivals is the bullfight called *dhiri*. Much less bloodthirsty than the Spanish version, a *dhiri* is fought between two thoroughbred bulls who lock horns in a test of strength and endurance. There is great excitement among the spectators, and gambling on the outcome.

Football v. cricket

Otherwise, the national sport in Goa is football – unlike the rest of cricket-mad India. That reflects the Portuguese influence, in contrast to British. It's said that football is in the blood of Goans, and music is in their hearts.

Music and folk dancing is the most popular entertainment open to visitors, who will otherwise find very limited nightlife. There is enormous range of colourful performances that reflect the cultural diversity of Goa: a full range of classical Hindu music and temple dancing; folk music and dances from the villages; centuries-old songs, dances and costume direct from Portugal; and a post-Independence fusion of ethnic and western music.

Some shows are presented on river cruises, as part of a sightseeing package, with guitars as the most popular instrument. Others are linked with a Goan meal in a traditional setting. It all makes a memorable few hours, with ample opportunity for flash photography. At most of the shows, an MC explains the action. For dance-happy spectators, there's often the chance of trying out steps with the performers.

3.9 Quick facts – all-India, and Goa

Total land area: 1,150,000 sq miles – just over half the size of Europe, or 1/3 of USA (*Goa: 1,400 sq miles – the size of Cornwall, or Rhode Island*).
Coastline: 4,350 miles (*Goa: 65 miles*).
Natural resources: coal (fourth-largest reserves in the world), iron ore, manganese, mica, bauxite, titanium ore, chromite, natural gas, diamonds, crude oil, limestone (*Goa: iron ore*).
Population: 930 million estimate, growth rate 1.9%. (*Goa: 1.2 million, growing faster through migration from other States*).
Life expectancy: 57 years male, 59 years female.
Total fertility rate: 3.7 children per woman.
Religion: Hindu 83%, Muslim 11%, Christian 2%, Sikh 2%. (*Goa: Hindu 60%, Catholic 37%*).
Literacy: male 62%, female 34%. (*Goa: over 77%*).

Language: Hindi, English, and 14 other official languages; another 24 languages spoken by at least a million people each. (*Goa: Konkani and Marathi; also English and Portuguese*).

Administrative divisions: 25 States and 7 Union Territories.

Independence: 15 August 1947 from UK (*Goa: 1961 from Portugal, and became the 25th State of the Union on 30 May 1987*).

Legal system: based on English common law.

National holiday: Anniversary of the Proclamation of the Republic, 26 January.

Suffrage: universal at age 18.

India's economy: 67% of India's population are engaged in farming, accounting for 30% of GDP. India is now self-sufficient in food grains and a net agricultural exporter, thanks to improved farming methods and use of new seed varieties. However, the green revolution has still not reached millions of villagers who continue to live in deep poverty.

Manufacture ranges from traditional handicrafts to factory production, much out-dated but with some modernisation and switch to high-tech industries. Business is subject to numerous government controls, though there are moves to liberalisation. Annual growth has averaged 4% to 5% during the past decade, with especially strong growth in services. Ongoing problems include 10% inflation, diminished foreign exchange reserves, and a large national debt.

Chapter Four

Goa sightseeing

4.1 Old Goa

Five miles up the Mandovi River from present-day Panaji, Old Goa once ranked among the wealthiest cities of India. Famed in early Hindu history and legend, Old Goa came under Muslim rule in the late 13th century, and became a major port of departure for Muslim pilgrims from India to Mecca.

But the big turning point came on November 25, 1510, when a Portuguese army under Afonso de Albuquerque conquered the city and massacred all the Muslim inhabitants. In this crucial battle, the Portuguese were very heavily out-numbered. They attributed their victory to divine help. As November 25 was the day of St Catherine of Alexandria (famed for her martyrdom on a wheel), the Portuguese decided their success came from the personal intervention of St Catherine. Hence they gratefully dedicated the Cathedral to her.

Goa was the first Portuguese territorial possession in Asia. Later it became the capital of all Portuguese territories in the East, with the same civic privileges as Lisbon.

By 1565 the city had become a major trading centre, handling the luxury exchange of goods between West and East – China, Persia and India. This was the age of 'Golden Goa'. Peak prosperity reigned from 1575 to 1625.

The cross followed the flag. From the early 16th century Goa became a Franciscan missionary base. St Francis Xavier came to Goa in 1542 and undertook the training of Jesuit missionaries. Goa became the principal Catholic missionary centre for the East, with jurisdiction over all Portuguese territories beyond the Cape of Good Hope.

In Goa itself, thanks to appropriate support from the Inquisition, inhabitants of the coastal areas were converted to Christianity. With the building of the magnificent Sé Cathedral, the Basilica of Bom Jesus, other churches, convents, colleges, a hospital and a one-acre Palace of the Inquisition, Old Goa was rated as the Rome of the East. Population rose to 200,000.

But the glory faded. The Portuguese came under pressure from the Dutch, British and French. Then followed epidemic and decay. In 1843 the seat of government was finally moved to present-day Panaji. Old Goa was abandoned, and fell into ruins. Only a few villagers now reside in what formerly was the greatest city of Portugal's Asian empire.

Old Goa today offers fascinating sightseeing. The masterpieces of 16th-century Portuguese architecture are well preserved in lonely splendour amid the remains. The body of St Francis Xavier, patron saint of Goa, is enshrined in a carved silver casket in the Basilica.

Certainly no holiday visit is complete without taking in the sights of Old Goa. Sightseeing tours can combine Old Goa with a circuit of the principal Hindu temples; or can be linked with spare time in Panaji, and possibly a sunset river cruise rounded off by a traditional evening meal. There are several options. Ask your rep what's on offer.

The principal approach to Old Goa – also known by its Portuguese name of Velha Goa – is along a 7-mile causeway built by the Portuguese in the 17th century. Previously the connection between the two cities was by boat. On the left is the River Mandovi; on the right, a broad area of salt pans, with a few water buffaloes grazing alongside.

It's a beautiful drive, looking across to Chorao Island. Part of that island is dedicated to a bird sanctuary with lush vegetation that encourages coots, grey herons, egrets, kingfishers, brahminy ducks, sandpipers and the migratory pintail. Around 180 species have been recorded.

Along the tidal mudflats some of these birds can be seen from the road. Portuguese-style villas facing the river are shaded by coconut palms.

The two great monuments of Old Goa – the gleaming-white Cathedral and the reddish-brown Basilica – face one another across a square. The entire green-lawn area is a World Heritage Site. "Anyone who causes damage can get three months in gaol and/or a fine of up to 5,000 Rs."

The Basilica of Bom (Good) Jesus contains the tomb and mortal remains of St Francis Xavier who in 1541 was responsible for spreading Christianity throughout the Portuguese colonies in the East.

The basilica is built on a cruciform plan of red laterite stone, combined with a cement-coloured stone which is schist. Construction took only 11 years, from 1594. The white building alongside is a guest house, with accommodation for the priests.

Inside the basilica, the main features are a 17th-century richly gilded main altar, a statue above of St Ignatius of Loyola (founder of the Jesuit Order), a fantastic pulpit of carved teak, and the Italian silver casket where most of St Francis Xavier is displayed. His right arm is in St Peter's, Rome.

The casket was installed in 1637, but the marble mausoleum – the 10-year work of a Florentine sculptor Giovanni Foggini – was not finished until 1698. The anniversary of the saint's death, December 3, is a public holiday. Every tenth year his casket is lowered for a six-week period, so that pilgrims can have a closer look. This event is scheduled from 21 November 1994 until 7 January 1995.

In the annexe, oil paintings depict scenes from St Francis Xavier's life, and there's an art gallery upstairs. Birds nest and twitter in the cloisters.

Sé Cathedral is the largest in Asia, built between 1562 and 1652 in Portuguese Gothic style. Originally there were towers each side of the West Door, but one collapsed in 1776. The remaining tower houses a famous bell, often called the Golden Bell because of its rich sound.

Formerly the bell tolled whenever the Inquisition was pronouncing public sentence on heretics and sinners in a solemn ceremony – an *auto-da-fé* ('act of faith'). For those who repented, the judges ordered suitable penance. Obstinate heretics who refused to confess were handed over to the secular authorities for immediate burning at the stake. The bell still rings daily, but not for bonfires.

The cathedral took 90 years to build, from 1562 till 1652. The altar is dedicated to St Catherine of Alexandria. A carving on the bottom row, centre, of the altar depicts the saint with her wheel of martyrdom. The 16th-century organ is still in working condition and is played regularly.

One of the side chapels has a baroque entrance gate with intricate carving. Within is a cross which reputedly has healing properties, and is therefore the object of veneration and pilgrimage.

Goa's best examples of Portuguese religious art are in the adjoining convent and church of St Francis of Assisi. Rebuilt from a mosque in 1521, it contains gilded woodcarvings and beautiful murals. The floor is made of carved gravestones. Round the back is an Archaeological Museum.

Of historical interest is the Viceroy's Arch, which celebrates the Portuguese conquest of the city. It was erected by Francisco da Gama, who was the governor from 1597 to 1600. He erected the monument in memory of his great-grandfather, the explorer Vasco da Gama, whose statue looks out to sea. From the neighbouring landing stage, a ferry crosses to Divar Island.

4.2 Temples

The Portuguese occupation of Goa came in two waves. The first four coastal districts to be subdued in the early 16th century were known as the 'Old Conquests' (Velhas Conquistas). Later the Portuguese mastered seven more districts in the more hilly inland areas - the 'New Conquests' (Novas Conquistas).

During the first wave, temples were destroyed, to be replaced by churches. Persuasion ensured that most of the occupied population became Christian.

Many Hindus retreated from coastal and river-bank areas to the relative safety of the foothills, where they re-established new shrines and temples, especially in Ponda district.

The pattern has remained into the 20th century. Coastal areas are mainly Catholic, and the interior Hindu. The market town of Ponda is the centre of numerous Hindu shrines. Several of Goa's main temples can easily be visited in a sightseeing tour that includes beautiful scenery and traditional Hindu villages.

Against a lush backdrop of paddy fields, palm trees, woodlands and green hills, the temples add another brilliant touch to the colour scheme. Their architecture is distinctive, with a standard layout to each complex. Outside the main entrance gate is a sacred water tank for ritual bathing. A tall lamp tower called a Dipa-Stambha overlooks the precincts. Guest rooms called Agrashalas for pilgrims are ranged around the inner courtyard.

Shri Manguesh Temple – Along a road towards Ponda, in a beautiful setting of terraced hillsides, coconut palms and mango trees, the temple's elegant white lamp tower stands out on a hilltop. The local village has a serene atmosphere. Meeting the needs of the pilgrim trade which brings thousands of visitors every year, there's a line of souvenir stalls, kiosks, and people selling sun-hats and fruit.

Leading up to the welcome gate, lines of women and children offer lotus garlands for a rupee or two. It's hard to resist hanging some around your neck.

This temple is dedicated to the Goddess Parvati, the heavenly consort of Lord Siva. Like many Hindu temples elsewhere in the territory, Shri Manguesh shows signs of Portuguese influence. The interior, for instance, is fitted with Portuguese chandeliers. The surrounding courtyard with two-storied accommodation for pilgrims looks remarkably like a south-European medieval monastery in plan, colouring and details. The window grilles, for example, are pure Portuguese in style.

Shri Shantadurga Temple – Dedicated to the Goddess of Peace, this temple dates from year 1728, and is located at the foothill of Kavalem near Ponda. Every day at one p.m. a religious ceremony is held with the inner shrine illuminated by reflected sunlight, directed by a mirror.

4.3 Panaji

This pleasant whitewashed city on the south bank of the Mandovi River became the Goan capital last century. Many of the building materials were floated down-river from the abandoned city of Old Goa. The town reflects its Portuguese heritage.

The most important monument is the Secretariat building, once a Muslim Palace then a Portuguese Fort. The Portuguese governor-generals moved here from Old Goa in 1760, and it remained their official palace until a royal decree in 1843 also made it the seat of government.

The gleaming white building faces the river, with a few antique cannons as reminder of the historic past. Alongside is a small park that centres on a dramatic statue of the Abbé Faria, who is claimed as the founder of hypnosis by suggestion. He was born 1756, and died in Paris 1819. He was immortalised in the novel by Alexandre Dumas, *The Count of Monte Cristo*.

A stroll along the quayside towards the river mouth takes one past several pleasure boats that offer afternoon and evening cruises with Goan folk entertainment. Fishing boats cluster together, and there's the constant sight of rusty barges, laden with iron ore for international export through Mormugao.

A crowded but minimum-cost ferry operates a regular service across the river, but there are two bridges just a mile or two upstream. Previously there was one newly-built bridge which fell down. Now they have two bridges side by side, presumably 'just in case'.

These bridges are the only direct road link between north and south Goa.

The best view over the city's red-tiled rooftops is from the Altinho hill above Panaji, where delightful houses and gardens are located.

A focal point of the city centre is the 16th-century Church of the Immaculate Conception, a dazzling white cathedral which stands out beautifully against the skyline, with a dramatic stairway to the entrance.

As Goa's commercial and administrative centre, Panaji also features shops that are well stocked with a wide selection of local products. Much of the original Portuguese character still remains, including numerous low-life taverns.

Although English has virtually taken over, some shop signs still cling to their Portuguese fascia boards. You can choose, for instance, between the Berberia Real (Royal Barber Shop) and a rival called the Friends Haircutting Saloon.

4.4 Countryside, crops and spices

One of the pleasures of Goa is the ease of seeing first-hand the life of village India, which often is only a few minutes' walk from your resort hotel.

On sightseeing excursions to markets, churches or temples, the cross-country journeys are packed with still more interest: an ever-changing panorama of village scenes, people, farming and gorgeous scenery.

It's possible to dig deeper, taking a closer look at rural India than is possible from behind an air-conditioned window. There are jeep safaris available, short on comfort but long on atmosphere. You can explore little dirt tracks where no other westerners go, and then finally arrive at a beach where the jeep party is totally on its own.

Another option is based on a demonstration of country crafts such as processing the rice harvest, or watching toddy tappers at work (see page 39), or seeing how spices are grown. Some of these tours are rounded out with an ethnic meal, or folk music and dance performances.

There's much more to rural Goa than subsistence farming. Employment patterns are changing as more people move away from traditional fishing, farming, forestry and mining in favour of the service industries, especially tourism. Eleven small industrial estates have been established near villages, to foster small manufacture and labour-intensive cottage industries. High educational standards in Goa – second only to Kerala in literacy rating – makes it easier for Goans to learn new skills.

The villages themselves have great charm, normally focussing either on a whitewashed church or a multi-coloured Hindu temple. Virtually every village house has a kitchen garden that grows vegetables such as okra, capsicum, chillies, aubergines, garlic and pumpkins. The yellow pumpkin flowers are also chopped into a vegetable. Country chickens wander around, free-range.

Flowers are everywhere, with bougainvillaea rampant. Women and schoolgirls walk along with a single flower in their hair or garlands of lotus blossoms.

Useful trees border the villages: tamarind, jackfruit, mango and papaya. At village ponds, water buffaloes come for a drink with egrets in close attendance, while kingfishers flit amid the water lilies. Everything is green, thanks to the torrential rains of June till late September. In flat areas, rice paddies are backed by coconut groves.

Generally, rice is a once-a-year crop, raised during the monsoon months. Where irrigation is available, two crops are possible. On some terraced fields they plant okra and cucumbers during the monsoon.

Plots which are used for rice paddies during the rains are planted with green vegetables and beans after the harvest. These crops need less moisture, and grow well during the remainder of the year.

The hills are a beautiful feature of Goa, with winding roads and lush green foliage. Many slopes are terraced, or planted with fruit trees. Here and there the reddish laterite rock is quarried, and cut into blocks for house construction. A tougher form of this laterite was used in building the Basilica and other monuments in Old Goa. The colouring is a reminder that Goa's most lucrative export is iron ore, delivered in huge quantities especially to Japan.

Even the steepest hills can support plantations of fruit and nut trees. Typical are the 50-ft betel nut trees, with pineapples growing in their shade.

Betel-chewing

From the totally different betel vine comes the small leaves that are used as an envelope for 'pan', a paste of betel nut, lime and spices. Pan is chewed after meals as a digestive aid and breath sweetener, causing a brick-red saliva which stains the lips, mouth and gums. This betel-chewing custom is spread widely throughout India.

Villagers take pride in their mangoes, which are very high in sugars. In the heat of May, when mangoes are fully ripe, they can rot in three days. The Goans gorge themselves during that harvest season, but also produce large quantities of mango juice as a year-round thirst-quencher. They convert surplus mangoes into chutney or jam.

The most interesting fruit is the cashew, "the money plant of Goa". Cashew nuts are Goa's leading cash crop and currency earner. The trees were originally introduced by the Portuguese to halt erosion on hillsides which were useless for rice terracing. Once the trees are planted, they need very little attention. There is enough monsoon rain to ensure ideal growing conditions.

The fruit itself is roughly pear-shaped, but smaller, while the nut hangs down *outside* the fruit – a unique arrangement! There's no need to climb the trees for harvesting during the February to May season. Villagers wait until the red and yellow fruits actually drop – when fully ripe – and merely have to pick them up. Apart from domestic use, the cashew nuts go to factories for processing, ready for local sale and export.

The cashew fruit is dripping with juice. Open it with care, otherwise your clothes will be drenched! It has a reasonable flavour, and smells rather like mango. Some attempts have been made to bottle the juice, but it has not taken off in popularity. Instead it is used as a base for the alcohol called feni.

Villagers tread the semi-liquid pulp in traditional style, and store the juice in barrels for a few days' natural fermentation. The wine-like liquid is then poured into earthenware pots, and a fire lit underneath. Through a primitive pipe, distilled alcohol drips into a smaller vessel. In this raw state, the cashew urrack is a popular village drink. Otherwise the product is sold to bottling plants for a second distillation, to produce a smoother feni that sells in liquor shops for 50 or 60 Rs per bottle.

A similar product is coconut-palm feni made from distilled toddy. With Goa's large plantations of coconut trees, toddy-tapping can be almost a full-time job. Men climb the coconut palms barefoot, using the tree rings as a toe-hold.

The sweet colourless sap can be an instant thirst-quencher, or allowed to ferment into a low-alcohol beverage, or distilled into a straight liquor.

Formerly, toddy was used in bread-making, because it was high in yeast. But that use has now discontinued. Toddy vinegar, however, is still an essential part of the Goan kitchen – used in vinda-lho dishes, for instance.

Model spice farm

An award-winning spice and fruit farm at Khande-par in Ponda District is open to visitors. It's a man-made Garden of Eden, except for no apple trees. In this model 50-acre farm, the owners have planted specimens of every fruit or spice-bearing tree or shrub grown in Goa and neighbouring states.

Ornamental plants also have been given space. Experiments and techniques used on the estate attract study groups of farmers, who also take home saplings and cuttings of new varieties.

Typically, the owners use organic methods to produce an average yield per tree of 120 coconuts a year compared with the Goan average of 80. Dwarf trees, with smaller nuts, yield 250 compared with the State average of 140.

Interplanting with spice trees and bushes is another key to improved land use, though many of the spices are normally field crops. You can see first-hand how some well-known spices are grown and processed.

Cloves grow best in Kerala, which supplies 90% of India's total production. Goan climate is not moist enough in comparison with Kerala, which gets two rains a year.

Nutmeg trees likewise grow better in the moister conditions of Kerala. Trees are eight years old before starting to yield a crop. When mature, a tree bears over 1,000 nuts per year.

Cinnamon is one of the easiest trees to grow. Stick a cutting in the ground, and a year later it has flourished and the bark is ready for harvesting in the form of cinnamon sticks.

Black Pepper grows on vines which cling to coconut trees, so that two crops come from the same piece of ground. Each vine yields 1½ kilos of black pepper. The vine is similar to the one producing betel leaves.

All-spice trees are native to Kerala, but are being grown in Goa as an experiment. The berries give some of the aroma and flavour of all spices.

4.5 Birdlife

There are 250 breeds of birds in Goa, of which an alert bird-watcher should spot at least fifty during a holiday. Even for a less dedicated enthusiast, it's worth packing binoculars for the added pleasure of taking a closer look at Goa's birdlife. Here are some birds to expect.

Black drongo or **king crow** – is the one with very long, deeply forked tail, likes perching on telephone lines.

Blue-tailed bee-eater – seen at the edge of the beach.

Brahminy kite – very common, scavenging around lakes and villages, very distinctive when in flight.

Brown-headed gull – looks like a blackheaded gull but is bigger.

Cattle egrets – snow-white birds, usually standing on or near cattle to feed on insects.

Chiffchaff – same as the British bird.

Common sandpiper – wades in rock pools.

Common iora – greenish or yellow-green plumage.

Coucal – lives in shrubs and on the ground.

Golden oriole – We always think it's wonderful to see one in Britain, but here they are hanging off every tree.

Hooded crows – unwanted, and unloved.

House sparrows – the first birds you see on landing at the airport.

Indian robin – black with a red band.

Koel – goes whoop-whoop-whoop.

Large pied wagtail – seen around flowing water, and takes rides on river ferry-boats.

Lesser golden-backed woodpecker – bright golden-yellow and black, with red crest.

Little stint – seen on the beach.

Little egret – has yellow feet and black bill, living at water's edge.

Magpie-robin – looks like a miniature magpie but its tail is cocked up. A good singer.

Mynah – several varieties, usually seen in small groups, flying between palm trees, occasionally perched high.

Paddy bird or **pond heron** – difficult to see when settled, but easily spotted in flight due to the flash of its distinctive white wings.

Pariah kites – dark brown plumage, forked tail easily seen in flight.

Plovers – lots of golden plovers, and parties of about a hundred little sand plovers in a field.

Purple-rumped sunbird – black or brown above, yellow below.

Ruff-dove – looks like a British pigeon.

Rufous-backed shrike – watches its territory from a conspicuous perch.

Spotted dove – recognised by white-spotted black collar.

White-breasted kingfisher – usually seen by hotel pools, catching fish and insects, and is happy on lawns.

White-backed munia – about the size of a blackbird, and is half-black and half-white down its chest.

White-browed bulbul and **redvented bulbul** – cheerful and noisy, always chattering.

Yellow-cheeked tit – has a black crest.

Chapter Five

Food and drink

5.1 Goan cuisine

Thanks to former occupations by Muslims and Portuguese, Goa offers a wide range of cuisine that includes Indian, Goan, Portuguese, Chinese, vegetarian and non-vegetarian.

In major hotels and restaurants, a choice of cuisines is offered, but of course the chefs have more skill in cooking their familiar local dishes. Part of the holiday experience is to sample the full flavour of Goan cuisine.

Outside the hotels, Goa has relatively few first-class eating places. However, most beaches feature very basic shack restaurants which offer refreshments, snacks, Goan dishes and seafood.

They are much cheaper than the hotels, but their standards of hygiene are dubious in the absence of running water or adequate toilet facilities.

We suggest you try the hotel dining rooms before venturing to eat outside. Hotel kitchen standards are now generally fairly high. But in rural districts or shack restaurants beware of salads, raw vegetables and soft fruits.

South Indian food is hotter than in northern India, and leans much more towards vegetarian dishes, using grains and lentils besides the staple rice. However, some Indian vegetarians eat seafood, on the basis that fish is 'fruit of the sea'.

Goan food in hotels is normally served medium spiced – enough to make them interesting, but not so hot as in home cooking. The scarlet chillies are cooled down by adding more coconut (which is fattening).

Ethnic tableware

To be completely authentic, Goan food is served on banana leaf plates, with coconut utensils. If you go all the way and eat with your fingers, remember that only the right hand should be used for putting food in your mouth. In the Indian culture, the left hand is reserved for other bodily needs.

Goans are specially fond of seafood which is prepared by different communities in different ways. According to a typical menu, seafood is supplied "Fresh with the spirit of the ocean." Prices depend on season and size. You can choose to have your fish fried with granulated rice, with masala gravy, stuffed or tandoori.

Some of the local fish names are not recognised by an English dictionary, and it's hard to find exact translations of seafood such as chomak, raons, modso or muddoshyo (lady fish). But one can feel amid more familiar territory when there's mackerel on the menu, or sardines, kingfish, grouper, squid, mullet and the well-known shellfish.

The temptation with shellfish is that it's so fresh and plentiful that it's easy to over-indulge. At a shack restaurant, prawns with rice may cost only 30 Rs. In a well-known Panaji restaurant, a Prawn Sukem costing 70 Rs is billed as a spicy mixture of prawns with onions and coconut.

Vegetarian dishes are delicious, hot and non-greasy, enlivened with freshly ground spices. Curries are varied in content and strength but always fried in ghee (a kind of clarified butter) and served with rice. Side helpings of dal (pulses), pickles or curd-based dishes help soothe the palate.

Biryani is the generic name for numerous dishes based on fried rice – also known as pulav – often flavoured or coloured with turmeric or saffron. There are chicken biryanis, mutton, prawns, or vegetable.

India generally is no place for a dedicated meat-lover, and Goa is no exception. It's much better to stay with fish. However, something unusual for India is that Goan Christians eat numerous pork dishes, many disguised as sausages. That could be the main Portuguese contribution to the Goan menu.

Baker's basket

Breads are available in great variety. Podhers – bakers – start selling bread from 5 a.m., with baskets strapped to their bicycles. They announce their arrival by sounding a horn. Their stock normally includes:

Kankonn – Hard crisp bread shaped like a bangle, and usually dipped in one's morning tea.

Poie – A thick chapati-type bread that can be halved, to be stuffed with meat or vegetables.

Sanna – Steamed rice bread steeped in coconut toddy, with a sweetish taste. Can be eaten alone, or dipped in gravy.

Unde – Crusted round bread with a slit on top.

Breakfast dishes

An effective way to counteract digestive problems is to start each day with some natural yoghourt (sometimes known as 'cura'). Other breakfast specialities include 'idlis' (steamed rice dumplings), vadais (deep-fried savoury doughnuts) and dosais (wafer-thin rice pancakes). They each come in dozens of varieties and flavours. Masala dosais, for instance, are filled with a spicy mixture of potatoes fried with onion.

5.2 Goan menus

To help you interpret Goan menus, with some clue to the ingredients, here are some guidelines.

Ambot Tik – A sour and pungent paste usually stuffed into shark, squid, electric ray or catfish. It is one of the few preparations made without coconut, and is best served with rice.

Chicken or mutton do piaza – Cooked in gravy with lots of onions.

Chicken Cajreal – Chicken marinated in a preparation of chillies, ginger, garlic and lime. Grilled, roasted or griddled, it is served with a salad and squeezed lime.

Chourisso – Spicy pork sausages, either boiled or fried with onions and chillies.

Dal – A lentil dish best tried with nan bread or chapatis.

Feijuado – A special sauce added to dry beans and local sausages.

Khatkhate – Diced bananas, sweet potatoes, pumpkins and carrots, cooked in a masala made of coconut.

Masala – A paste, such as ground chillies, with some sugar and toddy vinegar – added to a variety of dishes.

Mergolho – Prepared from pumpkin and papaya, cooked in coconut juice and milk masala.

Paneer steak – Cottage cheese steak grilled and served with curried sauce and rice.

Sorpotel – Diced pork liver, well fried and cooked in a toddy vinegar, medium spicy.

Vindalho – A pungent dish made of diced beef, pork or fish, added to a gravy with a base of garlic and a rich helping of toddy vinegar.

Xacuti – A preparation of coconut juice, grated and roasted coconut, and a variety of roasted spices, usually added to mutton.

Xec Xec – pronounced shek shek. A tasty crab dish made with grated coconut, garlic and ginger.

Desserts which are predominantly sweet:

Bebinca – A multi-layered coconut cake made from flour, egg yolks, sugar, coconut juice and nutmeg.

Bolinhas – small round cakes made of coconut and semolina, topped with a cherry.

Dodol – Rich in taste and made with jaggery (brown sugar that looks like cow-pats before it's broken down), coconut juice and nuts.

Neureos – Made of a paste of dough, stuffed with a mixture of grated coconut, cardamon seeds, sugar, nuts and raisins.

Perada – A guava cheese made either hard, or soft and sticky. Looks like solid treacle, and is very sweet.

5.3 All the drinks

The rule 'don't drink the tap water' applies rigidly in the Indian sub-continent. Jugs of purified water are supplied in hotel rooms, and tea, coffee and soft drinks are safe. But remember that the ice in drinks outside your hotel could be made from unpurified water. 'When in doubt leave it out'.

Bottled mineral water is available, costing 10 Rs a litre in supermarkets, and somewhat more in hotels and restaurants. A popular brand in Goa is called Bailley's. It's worth packing a vacuum flask, to keep the liquid cool during day trips.

Fresh fruit juices are sold everywhere from wayside kiosks, amd you may wish to try neera – coconut juice, good after too much of the local hooch called feni.

An especially refreshing drink is freshly squeezed lime juice and soda, with or without sugar. Buttermilk is also a tasty thirst quencher. Another local favourite is Lassi, a yoghourt based drink. Besides tasting good, it's an excellent stomach settler should you have any problems.

At most places of interest, vendors sell cold factory-bottled soft drinks. These are quite safe, but it's a good idea to carry some drinking straws with you, to avoid using some of the dubious drinking containers offered.

Popular brands are: Citra (7-Up); Miranda (orange); Limca (bitter lemon); and Thums Up (local Cola).

Some shack restaurants and refreshment kiosks offer sugar cane drinks, based on freshly mangled cane. In some places the vendors have moved into the 20th century with power-driven presses.

In contrast to the rest of India, commercially produced alcoholic drinks are freely sold in Goa at very reasonable prices in bottle stores. Dry white wines cost 55 Rs a bottle; sweet port wines – a Portuguese legacy – cost between 25 and 40 Rs.

In hotel bars and restaurants, Kingfisher beer or an Arlem Pilsner cost about 30 Rs for a 60-cc bottle; whisky and gin 25 Rs a 30-ml tot; small glasses of Golconda dry white wine for 15 Rs.

Everywhere in Goa you'll see advertisements for whisky, which mostly is produced in the neighbouring State of Karnataka. Typical brand-names are Black Knight, Director's Special, Black Stallion, Officers' Choice, Diplomat, Aristocrat, Royal Velvet and Royal Challenge.

These drinks mostly cost only 80 Rs a bottle in liquor stores, or 5 Rs for a 30-ml tot in a wayside bar plus another 3 Rs for soda. On a scale of ten for Scotch, connoisseurs rate Indian whisky around four. Local rum, vodka and gin are rated higher.

The Goans also produce their own local liquor – feni – distilled either from palm toddy or from cashew fruit. Feni tastes rather like raw slivovitz. Take a quick gulp, and it's like being shot in the throat. But double distilled feni, flavoured with cummin seeds or ginger, is much smoother. (See the previous chapter for more information on this popular village industry).

5.4 Fruits

Depending on the season, Goa offers a year-round supply of fruits: water melons, grapefruit, mangoes, pineapples, jackfruits, papayas, guavas, bananas, grapes and even a few custard apples (a fruit eaten with a spoon).

Beware of eating fruit which cannot be peeled.

● DELHI

Jaipur

Fatehpur Sikri

Agra

Bombay

Hyderabad

Goa

Bay of Bengal

Arabian Sea

Bangalore

Madras

INDIA

Sri Lanka

Colombo

| 0 | 100 | 200 | 300 |

miles

Chapter Six

Visit India's highlight cities

6.1 Delhi - apex of the Golden Triangle

Delhi is India's richest city in sightseeing potential and is the prime base for side trips to Agra and Jaipur – the so-called 'Golden Triangle'.

From south to north through the sprawling capital – now with 9 million population – historians and archaeologists count seven or eight distinct cities built by successive rulers. The first city was established around 1060 AD, though there is evidence of continuous settlement from the 3rd century BC. The great monuments range from the early Moslem period of 12th century onwards, through Moghul period (1526-1857), and thence to the buildings of modern Delhi.

A series of broad, tree-lined avenues and parks separates the teeming bazaars, temples and mosques of Old Delhi from the British-built administrative capital of New Delhi, with its India Gate memorial, government ministries, embassies and modern hotels in garden settings.

City tours are normally split to give half-day each for New and Old Delhi. Sightseeing of New Delhi is combined with many ancient remains including Jantar Mantar, the Qutb Minar and Humayun's Tomb.

Surrounded by ultra-modern office blocks, **Jantar Mantar** is a fantastic astronomical observatory built in 1724 during the reign of Maharajah Jai Singh II of Jaipur (1699-1743). He took a keen interest in astronomy, both eastern and western, and built similar structures at Jaipur and Varanasi. The red stone 'instruments' look like surrealistic sculptures, with graduated markings to take readings. The centrepiece is a sun-dial, 40 ft high.

A truly more modern sightseeing highlight – west of the central area of Connaught Place – is the **Lakshmi Narayan Temple**, a colourful Hindu temple built in 1938. It is often called **Birla Temple**, after the philanthropist who financed the construction.

Humayun's Tomb, built 1565, is the first major example of Mughal architecture, with an octagonal ground plan, lofty arches, pillared kiosks and a double dome. These details became a prototype for the Taj Mahal in Agra. There are rich photo opportunities, such as pictures of bullocks that power the lawnmowers. Visitors are waylaid by women with pots on their heads, all ready to pose for a modelling fee of five rupees. Snake-charmers tune up whenever a Westerner approaches.

The **Qutb Minar** is the tallest stone tower in India – a 13th-century landmark 240 ft high, visible for miles. The fluted minaret tapers gracefully from a base of 47 feet diameter to the summit which is a slender 8 feet.

Alongside the Qutb Minar is India's earliest surviving mosque, which translates as **The Might of Islam Mosque**. Completed in 1197, it was greatly enlarged by later rulers. Twenty-seven Jain and Hindu temples were demolished to provide building materials. The carved decorations blend Islamic and Hindu traditions.

A famous 5th-century **Iron Pillar** in the mosque courtyard shows not a trace of rust – a tribute to the skill of ancient India's metalworkers. By tradition, anyone who can reach backwards to clasp hands around the pillar will have good luck.

Old Delhi

The 7th city dates from 1638 when the Emperor Shah Jahan moved his capital from Agra back to Delhi. Former cities were demolished to build the magnificent red sandstone fort and extend the city walls to a circumference of over five miles. Five of the fourteen huge entrance gates still remain: Delhi Gate, Kashmiri, Turkman, Ajmeri and Lahori.

The Red Fort

Virtually a town in itself, the Fort covers a very large area. Some parts of the grounds are still fenced off as a military area. Deeper into the Fort, you pass through a gateway where tickets are sold for Sound and Light Shows. Be sure to return after dark for a staging of the great historical events that took place within the citadel walls.

In contrast to the teeming highways outside, the Fort is a delightful haven of tranquility. The buildings are low profile, most of them glistening white, set around green lawns bordered by floral displays. Indian women tourists themselves add a rich colour to the scene, with their flowing saris.

The palaces of the inner courtyard provide excellent perching and nesting places for the resident birdlife, like a gigantic aviary. From the palace balconies one can look down on snake-charmers who hope that coins and banknotes will flutter down in appreciation of the music and the swaying snakes.

Chandni Chowk

The historic Main Street of Old Delhi is a ceremonial avenue widened during Shah Jahan's reign for his glittering processions to Red Fort. In 17th century it became a street of great houses, jewellers and cloth merchants, who gave it a long-standing reputation as the world's richest thoroughfare. Today, the Imperial glory and wealth have gone, but the area remains rich in interest.

Much city life is lived in the open. Chapati sellers are surrounded by customers eating the pancake-style bread hot from the griddle. Men and children wash at street standpipes; barbers and their clients squat for an open-air shave; nimble-fingered flower sellers string garlands of blooms; cycle repairers festoon tree branches with tubes and tyres.

Virtually any time of the day, Chandni Chowk is totally clogged with cycle rickshaws, scooter-taxis, horse-drawn tongas, bullock-carts, gaily-painted trucks, taxis and private cars. Through the jam move the myriad, colourful characters of India – men pushing hand-carts; a one-stringed fiddle salesman, with day's stock balanced on his head as he walks along playing; the fortune-tellers, holy men, beggars, porters and countrymen.

Almost opposite the Red Fort is another of Shah Jahan's great buildings – the **Jama Masjid**, the largest and most beautiful mosque in India. Admission for non-Muslims is permitted every morning until noon, and from 14-16 hrs.

Further out past the Kashmiri Gate, the Grand Trunk Road leads to a 14th-century fortress area called **Feroz Shah Kotlah** – the historic fifth city of Delhi – famed for the 27-ton **Ashoka Pillar** dragged from 125 miles away. The pillar dates from 3rd century BC.

Shopping
Really determined shoppers could go bargain-hunting in Chandni Chowk, especially if they have well-sharpened haggling skills. Otherwise, Connaught Circus and Connaught Place in New Delhi offer a complete range of Indian products, with honest shipping by reputable firms. Even so, some bargaining is still necessary, except in the various State Industries Emporia which operate on a strictly fixed-price basis. Highly recommended is the Central Cottage Industries Emporium in Janpath.

6.2 Agra
Agra has far more to offer than just the Taj Mahal. Seat of the Moghul Emperors during 16th and 17th centuries, Agra rivals Delhi for historical background and awe-inspiring monuments; a great red-sandstone **Fort** with walls 1.5 miles around; palaces, mosques and royal tombs lavishly built with glistening white marble, and a fantastic wealth of inlay work with precious and semi-precious stones.

Although the **Taj Mahal** is totally familiar to most travellers, thanks to photos and paintings that make the royal tomb into one of the world's best-known monuments, the impact is still breathtaking.

Through a massive gateway, 100 ft high, the visitor gets his first view of the mausoleum that took 20,000 labourers and craftsmen 12 years to complete. Whether seen in daytime or by full moon, the Taj Mahal ranks as India's most fabulous sight.

Certainly Shah Jahan kept his vow to build the greatest memorial that the world had ever seen, in memory of his beloved wife Mumtaz Mahal, who gave him 14 children and then died in childbirth.

Outside the standard sightseeing circuit, there's great interest in visiting workshops where craftsmen still produce marble inlay and mosaic, using all the patience, skill and primitive-looking tools that built the Taj Mahal.

Evenings? It's worth taking a slow-paced ride around Agra, through shopping areas where stall-holders sit patiently cross-legged, listening to their radios and cassette-players. By the light of pressure lamps, food vendors prepare variegated stews, fried dishes and rice. With any luck, there'll be a joyous, noisy wedding procession. It's a reminder that Agra is much more than a city of monumental tombs!

6.3 Fatehpur Sikri

Twentyfour miles west of Agra, en route to Jaipur, is the 16th-century ghost capital of Fatehpur Sikri. The entire red-sandstone city was built in a six-year period, 1569-1575, during the reign of Emperor Akbar.

Nearly seven miles in circumference, the city featured a magnificent mosque and all the necessary buildings for a major palace: a Treasury, Mint, stables, audience halls, sleeping apartments, and even a group of rooms and passages where the Emperor could play hide-and-seek or blind-man's-buff with his court ladies. For another favourite game, the main courtyard was marked out in chessboard style, using dancing girls as live pieces.

An artificial lake was dug out, there were numerous wells and baths and variegated water works. The only snag was that the entire complex had to be abandoned within 14 years owing to failure of the water supply.

Today, the perfectly preserved city gives an unforgettable impression of an Emperor's lifestyle of 400 years ago.

6.4 Jaipur

Jaipur, 190 miles from Delhi, is one of India's most beautiful cities, with fine parks and gardens in the best Technicolor tradition. Except for the blue sky, everything is rose-pink. Even the villagers go cycling along in bright pink turbans.

Jaipur was laid out in city-grid blocks by its founder, Maharajah Jai Singh, in 1727. Main streets are precisely 110 feet wide, side streets 55 feet. The entire city is surrounded by a wall of pink sandstone, with eight main gates.

Camels lope in from the surrounding desert areas. At the main city crossroads, flower-sellers offer gorgeous garlands – about four feet of stringed marigolds for hanging round your neck. Close by, the honeycomb facade of the **Palace of the Winds (Hawa Mahal)** has all the most delicate fantasy of the East. It's a favourite photo subject.

The **City Palace** occupies one-seventh of the original walled area of Jaipur, with beautiful gardens and pleasure grounds. The main palace building is the 7-storey **Chandra Mahal**, which offers superb views from the top floor. Also within the grounds is **Jai Singh's Observatory**, which is even more ambitious than his Jantar Mantar in Delhi. The sun-dial is accurate to within two seconds.

Seven miles out of town is **Amber Palace**, the hill-top fortress residence of the Rajput kings for 600 years. At the foot of the steep hillside, modern visitors have the option of changing onto elephants for the last uphill half-mile into the Palace.

Thus the traveller can savour the great highlight of Indian tourism: clutching at the *howdah* rail as the elephant lurches through tall gateways and into the vast palace courtyard. It's really something to write home about: "Travelling like a maharajah!"

The Ganesh Pol gate leads into an inner court where the royal apartments look onto an ornamental garden. Ceilings and walls are covered in delicate mosaics and glass inlays. There are marble screens, and doors inlaid with ivory and sandalwood. That craftsmanship still flourishes in the Jaipur bazaars, famed throughout India for jewellery and gemstones. If you really know emeralds, buy in Jaipur.

6.5 Bombay

To experience a total contrast to Goa, Bombay is only a one-hour flight away. It's the second most crowded city of India, after Calcutta. Obviously the shopping potential is far greater than in Goa; and there are major points of sightseeing interest.

Among the most famous monuments is the **Gateway of India** – built 1911 in 16th-century style to commemorate a visit by King George V and Queen Mary. The Gateway is a popular tourist venue. Departure point for launches to Elephanta Island, the area is thronged with peddlers, snake-charmers and fruit-juice vendors.

Between the Gateway and Marine Drive is the heart of business India, which looks more like high-rise Manhattan. **Marine Drive** (now called Netaji Subhash Road) faces the Arabian Sea with prestige apartments and a green area of sport clubs where cricket is the big game.

Eveningtime, the Marine Drive is a favourite promenade for Bombay families, enjoying the sea breeze. **Chowpatty Beach** – almost deserted during daytime – springs into lively activity at sunset.

Close by, the **Aquarium** displays India's finest collection of tropical marine and fresh-water fish. **Jain Temple**, on top of Malabar Hill, gives a magnificent overall view of Bombay. Close by are the **Hanging Gardens**, built over a water reservoir, and the attractive **Kamala Nehru Children's Park**.

Mani Bhavan is the Mahatma Ghandi Memorial Museum in a house where India's political leader stayed frequently. The **Prince of Wales Museum**, founded 1905, houses one of India's finest collections of coins, miniatures, Nepalese art, antique firearms, archaeology and natural history.

Bombay's most popular excursion is by launch, six miles out of Bombay harbour to Elephanta Island, where mangrove trees fringe the shallow waters. A long flight of steps from the landing-stage reaches to the **Elephanta Caves**, where 7th-century rock-cut temples are dedicated to Lord Shiva. He is depicted as Creator, Protector and Destroyer. A visit gives a crash course in Hindu art, sculpture and mythology.

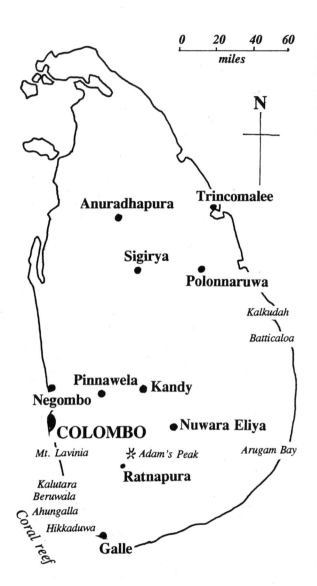

0 20   40   60
miles

N

Anuradhapura

Trincomalee

Sigirya

Polonnaruwa

Kalkudah

Batticaloa

Pinnawela Kandy

Negombo

COLOMBO

Nuwara Eliya

Mt. Lavinia ☀ *Adam's Peak* *Arugam Bay*

Ratnapura

Kalutara
Beruwala
Ahungalla
Coral reef *Hikkaduwa*

Galle

SRI LANKA

Chapter Seven

Sri Lanka

7.1 Enjoy your discoveries

Over the centuries, the island which hangs like a teardrop off the southern tip of India has had several changes of name. In 1972 Sri Lanka – meaning 'beautiful island' – reverted to its original name from 2,500 years ago, but was better known in more recent times as Ceylon.

Arab traders who came for spices and gem-stones called the island *Serendip*, which has contributed the word 'serendipity' to the English language – the faculty of making fortunate discoveries by accident. That derived from a Persian fairy-tale called *The Three Princes of Serendip*, in which the heroes possessed that gift. Visitors have enjoyed making their happy discoveries around the island ever since.

Geographically, Sri Lanka is more than just a teardrop in the ocean. North to south is 270 miles, and 140 miles at the widest across. That's somewhat larger than Eire, with mountains three times higher, rainfall about the same as west-coast Ireland, but with temperatures that stay firmly in the mid-80s F. Sea-bathing temperatures are likewise in the blissful 80s.

The island's recorded history of 2,500 years is highlighted by the monuments of ancient cities which are listed as World Heritage sites. Major archaeological discoveries are still being made, thanks to a 'Cultural Triangle' project jointly conducted by UNESCO and the local Archaeological Department.

The earliest settlers in Sri Lanka brought in the rice-growing techniques of India. Early kings of 5th century BC onwards gave the country great vitality and a well-ordered civilisation. Art and culture flourished with the advent of Buddhism as the island's main religion from 247 BC. Temples, monasteries, well-planned cities and palaces were built, while water engineers constructed a major system of irrigation reservoirs and canals. The foundations of today's Sri Lankan lifestyle comes in direct line from 2,000 years ago – in its principal religion, festivals, music, dance, serenity and gift for contemplation.

The Portuguese arrived in 1505 to capture a monopoly of the spice trade. They introduced Christianity to the west-coast areas under their control. They were ousted in 1656 by the Dutch, who were also interested in spices and a different brand of Christianity. In turn came the British in 1796, who gained complete control of the island with the capture of Kandy in 1815.

Britain's discovery was the plantation system, worked by low-cost Tamil labour from South India. Coffee was planted in the hill country, to be replaced by the far more successful tea industry. Rubber plantations spread in the foothills, and coconut groves along the coastal fringe. All these cash crops, and the rice for home consumption, contribute to the lush green scenery.

Exotic flora and wildlife flourish in the plains and highlands, and beside rivers, lakes and waterfalls. Protected rain-forests and national parks give added sanctuary to birds, 242 species of butterflies, and animals such as leopard, monkeys, deer and 2,000 wild elephants. The world's first nature reserve was established at Mihintale near Anuradhapura in the 3rd century BC, to uphold the Buddhist principle of forbidding man to kill any form of life. Over 2000 years later, Mihintale still doubles as a wildlife sanctuary and a centre of pilgrimage.

The great 20th-century happy discovery is the beaches. Hundreds of miles of golden sand encircle the island, with off-shore islets, lagoons and coral gardens, coves and bays. The coastal belt of palm trees ensures a green and shaded setting for the scattered plantations of holiday accommodation. All the watersport facilities are in place, with a total absence of crowds. From a beachside base you can enjoy making your own unexpected discoveries in this beautiful land.

7.2 Arrival & orientation

On arrival at Katunayake Airport, Colombo, go through passport control with your completed immigration card. Next stop is currency control where your currency card is stamped and must be surrendered on departure.

It's worth bringing in your limit of 1½ litres of spirits for emergency use, such as full moon days when no liquor is served. After collecting your baggage and clearing customs, exit the hall. Outside, tour reps await their clients. The agency for Thomson Holidays is Aitken Spence Travels, who will arrange transfer to hotels.

The airport is located 20 miles north of Colombo on Sri Lanka's west coast. The nearest resort is at Negombo, north of the airport. Most other beach resorts are spread along the coast, up to 50 miles south of Colombo.

7.3 At your service

Money: Currency taken into Sri Lanka should be declared on a Customs form which is then checked on departure. All exchange transactions should be recorded on the form.

The local currency is the Sri Lankan rupee (SL R), divided into 100 cents. Reckon around Rs.75 to the pound, or Rs.50 to the US dollar, subject to fluctuation.

Exchange facilities are available at the airport, but you can easily change money at your hotel. Banks are open Mon-Fri 9-13 hrs, and are closed weekends and all Bank Holidays including full moon days every month.

Well-known credit and charge cards are widely recognised by shops, hotels and restaurants. Some shops try to add a percentage. This is not acceptable, and complaint should be made to the card company.

At the Hong Kong and Shanghai Bank, 24 Sir Baron Jayatillake Mawatha, Colombo 1, holders of Visa and Access/Mastercard can obtain cash advances or purchase travellers cheques.

Transport: Bus services are possibly the cheapest in Asia, and among the most tightly packed. Trains are less crowded. Destination boards on buses and trains are in the national languages and in English. Generally, Western visitors prefer to use taxis or a self-drive car. The best bet for sightseeing are well-organised tours by coach or minibus.

Taxis are available and most are metered. Taxi drivers usually have enough English to get by. But make sure they clearly understand the destination required. Check that the 'flag' is turned down. If you intend to go a long distance, agree a price before setting off.

Car hire can be arranged through your representative. Driving in Sri Lanka demands a cool head, if only to avoid the suicidal goats and dogs but also the eccentric habits of cyclists and pedestrians. By western standards it costs relatively little extra to hire a driver with the car.

7.4 Colombo

A city tour of the Sri Lankan capital is easily arranged from any of the beach resorts. As the country's administrative and commercial centre, Colombo is a lively city of 500,000 population, located 20 miles from Katunayake International Airport.

Colombo has been a trading centre for centuries, dealing in pearls, gem-stones and spices, though Galle in the southwest corner was initially more important. The more recent settlers – Portuguese, Dutch and British – have all left reminders of their period of occupation.

The focal point of Colombo is called Fort. Originally built by the Portuguese to protect the harbour, Fort housed Portuguese and Dutch garrisons during the 16th to 18th centuries. The original walls have disappeared and only a couple of cannon remain.

Fort

Colombo's main expansion dates from the 19th century, when Britain converted the port into one of the world's largest artificial harbours. Today, Fort is the prosperous commercial heart of the city, where visitors can buy gems, brass and silverware.

Among the principal landmarks is the Lighthouse Clock Tower, built in 1837. In a spacious location opposite the gleaming white General Post Office is the former home of the colonial governors, now used as the President's House. Old Parliament Building, facing the Indian Ocean, houses the Presidential Secretariat.

A new Parliament complex of classical oriental design is located seven miles away at Sri Jayawardanapkura Kotte, the country's administrative capital.

Pettah

Adjoining Fort is Pettah, the city's teeming bazaar area which also includes numerous mosques, temples and Colombo's oldest Dutch church. Here is all the colour and chaos of the Orient. The Dutch Period Museum, at 95 Prince Street in the bazaar area, is a restored building – originally the Dutch town hall – with a peaceful courtyard. Train buffs could visit the Fort Railway Station for its collection of antique railway equipment.

Just south of Fort is Galle Face Green, a grassy promenade spread along a mile of seafront.

Three miles south of Fort is the fashionable area of Cinnamon Gardens – Colombo 7 – with spacious mansions and embassies. In this wealthy district is Vihara Maha Devi Park, more briefly known until the 1950s as Victoria Park. Flowering trees are ablaze with colour from March till early May. Close by, the National Museum – founded in 1877 – houses a wide collection of ancient sculpture and other relics.

Still further south is Dehiwala Zoo, where elephants have been trained to dance every afternoon at 17.15 hrs. Spread over a large area, the Zoo is well laid out and is rated among the best in Asia. Open 8-18 hrs daily.

7.5 Places to visit

Sri Lanka offers rich sightseeing. The principal highlights can be covered in a one-week circuit, especially to include the more distant historic sites such as Polonnaruwa, Sigiriya and Anuradhapura (around 130 miles from Colombo).

Otherwise, from the beach resorts of the southwest coast, a number of whole-day excursions are available, or longer trips which include overnight accommodation. They offer a good selection of the places visited on a more comprehensive tour. Ask your tour rep for details of the various itineraries.

Here's a short list of places worth visiting.

Ratnapura: High into the hill country, with magnificent scenery and views of 7300-ft Adam's Peak, Ratnapura lies about 40 miles inland from the coast. En route past paddy fields and towards the tea-planting areas are numerous gem-mining pits.

Ratnapura (meaning 'Gem City') is Sri Lanka's principal centre for the mining, cutting and polishing industries. The Gem Museum has a prized collection of blue sapphires, rubies, cat's eyes, amethysts, alexandrites, garnets, zircons and moonstones.

Adam's Peak, which dominates the skyline, is a pilgrimage site thanks to the huge 'sacred footprint' of Adam (or possibly Buddha or Lord Shiva). From Ratnapura, energetic devotees make a 7-hour climb by lamp-light to the mountain top, normally during the pilgrimage season of December to April. The aim is to watch the sunrise. Easier climbs start from the other side of the mountain, near the Dalhousie Tea Factory.

A visit to Ratnapura makes an excellent one-day trip from the coastal resorts. But longer tours continue to Nuwara Eliya and Kandy, past the prime tea gardens of the hill country.

Tea came to the economic rescue from 1867, after coffee was killed off by blight and spelt ruin for the estate owners. Plantation visits can show the field work of hand plucking, followed by the factory processes of withering, rolling, fermenting, drying and grading.

Nuwara Eliya: is a British-built hill station that would make Queen Victoria feel at home. Six thousand feet up, this summer retreat is fossilized in the old world charm of colonial days. There are Victorian tea planters' houses like in a prosperous English village, well-stocked trout streams, and one of Asia's best golf courses. Visitors should come prepared for rain and chilly evenings. The dramatic World's End viewpoint commands a sheer 3,500-ft drop to the valley below.

Kandy: More tea plantations can be seen en route to the former royal capital which fell to British troops in 1815. This ancient stronghold of the Sinhala kings is specially rich in cultural history. Dating from the centuries of royal patronage, the arts, crafts, music and dance still flourish.

The lakeside Temple of the Tooth (Dalada Maligawa) is dedicated to a Sacred Tooth of Buddha and is a holy shrine for all Sri Lankan Buddhists. Daily rituals with drums and flutes pay homage to the relic. A major 10-day festival – Procession of the Sacred Tooth – is held annually in July-August, with hundreds of dancers, drummers and 70 or more well-dressed and decorated elephants in the torch-lit parades.

The National Museum stands next to the Temple of the Tooth, in a building where the royal concubines were housed. Behind the Temple is the Archaeological Museum which occupies remnants of the royal palace.

Numerous other major temples, monasteries and meditation centres are located in and around Sri Lanka's second-largest city. Of special interest are the Royal Botanical Gardens at **Peradeniya**, just outside Kandy in a riverside setting. They were laid out in 1821 as the Kandyan queen's Pleasure Garden. Four hundred plant species are set in 150 acres.

Elephant Orphanage: From Kandy, some tours return to their coastal base with a pause to visit the Elephant Orphanage at **Pinnawela**, near Kegalle. Established twenty years ago, the Orphanage ranks as Sri Lanka's most popular elephant attraction, especially when it's mealtime in the nursery.

Longer tours of Sri Lanka continue north to another trio of ancient cities: Sigiriya, Polonnaruwa and Anuradhapura.

Sigiriya: The Rock Fortress, one of Sri Lanka's most spectacular sights, was built over 1500 years ago. This former royal citadel is decorated with voluptuous frescoes of bare-breasted women, still with colours glowing after 15 centuries. Scholars take pleasure in reading the graffiti of a thousand years ago, written in early Sinhalese script. Altogether it's a steep but rewarding climb.

Polonnaruwa: This remarkable ruined city was capital of the medieval Sinhalese kings who rose to power after the decline of Anuradhapura. The city reached its dazzling peak in the 12th century. The main sights are the sacred temples and the royal palace of King Parakrama Bahu the Great who ruled for 33 years; the carved rock statue of the King; and the giant stone Buddha carvings of Gal Vihara. The royal citadel was enclosed by walls 12 miles long by 21 miles wide - about the area of present-day London! The irrigation tank, known as the Sea of Parakrama, occupied over nine square miles.

Anuradhapura: As the island's most ancient religious centre, and the capital from 4th century BC to 10th century AD, Anuradhapura still ranks as a great pilgrimage centre. Buddhism was introduced in 247 BC, bringing cultural greatness to the island. The Sacred Bo Tree, decorated with gifts and frangipani, dates from the 3rd century BC, grown from a sapling of the original Bo Tree in northern India where Buddha found enlightenment.

The city was a model of civic planning, with separate areas for different social classes. Engineers built large reservoirs or 'tanks' to ensure a dependable water supply for domestic use and irrigation. Anuradhapura was finally abandoned, due to invasions from south India.

7.6 Shopping

Shops are open Mon-Fri 9-17 hrs, and many are also open Saturdays until 1 pm. Best buys are handicrafts, produced by traditional labour-intensive methods to high standards of design and workmanship.

Shopping for a full range of quality handicrafts can be done under one roof in stores operated by the Sri Lanka Handicrafts Board. These stores are located on York Street and at Liberty Plaza in Colombo, and in several tourist resorts and provincial centres.

The choice is bewildering: sterling and plated silverware, every imaginable object made of brass, lacquer ware, pottery and papier-mâché. There are highly decorative demon masks, wood-carvings, batik fabrics, handloom textiles, terracotta pottery, drums and flutes. Exquisite lace is produced by methods taught by the Portuguese in the 16th century.

Precious and semi-precious gems are Sri Lanka's most famous export: blue, yellow, pink, orange, white and star sapphires, rubies, cat's eyes, alexandrite, quartz, moonstones, zircons, garnets, amethysts and topaz.

The State Gem Corporation (Macan Markar Building, 24 York Street, Colombo) or the Ratnapura Gem Bureau guarantee the stones they sell, and are the most reliable outlets for the higher-priced stones. But hundreds of dealers can offer more moderately priced jewellery set with semi-precious gem-stones.

Unless you really know the business, don't listen to any sales pitch about buying stones in quantity for reselling at huge profit outside Sri Lanka.

Tea export is restricted to three kilos, any excess being subject to an export duty. The Tea Centre, operated by the Tea Promotion Board in Colombo at 574 Galle Road, sells special gift packages of selected brands.

All the spices mentioned in the next section are readily available, especially in Kandy and at the Peradeniya Botanic Gardens. Many private spice gardens are open to the public and sell direct.

7.7 *Eating out*

Resort hotels offer a full range of international cuisine. You will also find European, Chinese, Indian and Japanese restaurants, particularly in Colombo.

Sri Lankan cookery is spicy and exciting. Rice and red-hot curry is standard fare. Curries can include a complete alphabetical listing of spices: cardamon, chilli, cinnamon, clove, coriander, cummin, fenugreek, garlic, green ginger, mustard and pepper. Hotels soften the impact on their guests by toning down the chilli or increasing the base of coconut milk. If your mouth catches fire, douse the heat with buffalo-milk curds or chew some fresh coconut.

Seafood is particularly good. Lobster is expensive, but there is excellent choice of crab, prawn and squid, grouper, fresh tuna or trout. Meat dishes including buffalo are inexpensive, and are usually curried. Steaks are not recommended as local beef is usually tough.

Something different are pan hoppers – small rice pancakes that make a base for varied dishes from scoops of curry to honey and yoghourt. Fried egg hoppers are specially popular for breakfast; or you could spread plain hoppers with marmalade and butter, hoping the locals won't notice.

Sri Lanka is rich in its year-round variety of local fruit and vegetables, thanks to tropical conditions in the lowlands and a temperate climate in the highlands. Papaya, pineapple, banana and mango are always available, with refreshment from king-coconut juice. Other fruits such as mangosteen, avocado pear, durian, rambuttan, passion fruit, oranges and grapefuit are harvested mainly between July and August.

A number of rice-flour desserts are sweetened with palm treacle, which tastes something like maple syrup.

Thirst-quenchers: Don't drink tap water. Bottled water is safer, while the filtered water in hotel-bedroom flasks should cause no upsets. Imported canned drinks are available, but can be expensive.

Of course Coca-Cola is there, and a local imitation called Elephant House – a brand-name which appears on other soft drinks. There's also lemonade and ginger beer.

The country's own home brew is arrack, a high-octane distilled coconut toddy which can readily be mixed with soft drinks. Beer is also locally produced – a Pilsner type, low in alcohol. But you can also buy imported lagers. A hotel beer will cost roughly Rs.50, or gin and tonic Rs.30. Away from your hotel, avoid ice in your drinks.

Tea, of course, is everywhere, usually served very strong. Sample the different types, to decide which brands you wish to take home.

7.8 Nightlife

The big hotels feature dinner dancing, an occasional floor show, and sometimes a cultural performance of Kandyan dances or devil dancing. Check with newspapers or hotel desks for details.

Colombo has some steamy night clubs. Otherwise pack some good books.

7.9 Quick facts

Total area: 25,630 sq miles – the size of Southern Ireland, or half the size of New York State.
Coastline: 837 miles.
Time: GMT plus 5½ hrs.
Natural resources: limestone, phosphates, gemstones.
Land use: arable land 16%; permanent crops 17%; meadows and pastures 7%; forest and woodland 37%; other 23%.
Population: 18,000,000, growth rate 1.2%
Life expectancy: 69 years male, 74 years female.
Fertility rate: 2.3 children born per woman.
Ethnic groups: Sinhalese 74%, Tamil 18%.
Languages: Sinhala, Tamil and English.
Religion: Buddhist 69%, Hindu 15%, Christian 8%, Muslim 8%.
Work force: 6,600,000; farming 46%, mining and industry 13%, commerce and transport 12%, services etc 28%.

Literacy: 86% – male 91%, female 81%.
Capital: Colombo, population 660,000.
Independence: 4 February 1948 (from UK).
Government: a democratic socialist republic.
Legal system: a blend of English common law, Roman-Dutch, Muslim and customary law.
Executive branch: president, prime minister, cabinet.
Judicial branch: Supreme Court.
Political parties: United National Party (UNP), Sri Lanka Freedom Party (SLFP) and others with smaller support.
Suffrage: universal at age 18.

The economy: inflation and unemployment are high, but economic conditions are improving. Plantation crops, gemstones and textiles are the main currency earners.

Farming: occupies almost half the workforce, with tea, rubber and coconuts yielding 35% of export earnings. Other crops include rice, sugarcane, pulses and spices.

7.10 Festivals and public holidays

A great delight for visitors to Sri Lanka is the number of public holidays and festivals – around 30 days a year – though it can be most frustrating for a business traveller. Quite apart from the weekend breaks, there are some secular or political holidays:

Jan 14 – Tamil Tahi Pongal harvest festival day
Feb 4 – Independence Day
April – Two days' Sinhala and Tamil New Year
May 1 – May Day
May 22 – National Heroes' Day
Dec 31 – Special Bank Holiday

In addition, all the principal Buddhist, Hindu, Christian and Moslem religious holidays are kept as public holidays, including Easter, Christmas, the end of Ramadan and Mohammed's birthday.

Besides all these, every full moon day is a holiday, called *poya*, when all places of entertainment are closed and no liquor is sold. Hotels make special arrangements for guests to give their drink orders on the previous day. If Monday or Friday are poya days, many local people take off on long weekend trips, crowding the transport and accommodation facilities.

Virtually every month sees at least one or two highly colourful Buddhist or Hindu festivals, which are fascinating for visitors. Because of dependence on the moon, dates shift from year to year. Check the calendar when you arrive!

7.11 Hints and useful addresses

Security: There is long-standing conflict between the Sri Lankan government and a Tamil extremist group, the Liberation Tigers of Tamil Eelam (LTTE). Military actions may continue in northern and eastern areas of the island, where travel restrictions are enforced. Wilpattu and Galoya National Parks are considered unsafe. These locations are far removed from the international resort areas.

Electricity: 230/240 volts AC, 50 Hz. Round 3-pin plugs are usual, with bayonet lamp fittings.

Telephone: To avoid the usual hotel mark-ups on international phone calls, buy a Payphone Card which can be used from public phones.

From abroad, the dialling sequence for Sri Lanka is (010 from UK) +94 followed by area code and the local number.

Dress: When entering a temple or monument, visitors should remove shoes. It's useful to take along a pair of socks, as the ground can burn the soles of your feet. You are not allowed to visit some temples in shorts.

Elsewhere, informality is the rule, but swimwear should be worn only by the pool or on the beach. Topless and nude bathing is banned! Lightweight cotton clothing is ideal for the climate, but pack a sweater and medium weight slacks for the hill country. An umbrella is useful for the occasional shower – or even for sightseeing in the open sun.

Departure: Individual travellers must pay an airport departure tax of Rs.500, which is settled direct by some tour operators such as Thomson Holidays. At check-in and security, the luggage search is manual and thorough. There's a bank for changing any left-over local currency, which may not be taken out of Sri Lanka. A duty-free shop, cafeteria, bar and shops are located on the airport's first floor, using foreign currency only.

Photography: Visitors are welcome to take snaps of Buddha statues and other religious images. But do not drape yourself alongside them, nor expect the saffron robed Buddhist monks to pose for a picture.

Tipping: A service charge is generally included in your bill, and tipping is optional. It's advisable to carry small change if you want to tip guides when sightseeing.

Useful addresses:

Sri Lankan Tourist Board (UK), 13 Hyde Park Gardens, London W2 2LU.
Tel: (0171) 262 5009 or 262 1841. Fax: 262 7970.
Open Mon-Fri 9-17 hrs.

High Commission for the Republic of Sri Lanka, 13 Hyde Park Gardens, London W2 2LU.
Tel: (0171) 262 1841.

Sri Lankan Embassy, 2148 Wyoming Avenue, N.W., Washington, D.C. 20008. Tel: (202) 4834 025/8. There's a Sri Lankan Consulate in New York, and honorary consulates in Los Angeles, New Orleans and Newark.

Addresses in Colombo
Tourist Information Centre, 321 Galle Road, Colombo 3. Tel: 573175.
Gives advice on Sri Lankan culture, customs, history, etc. Open Mon-Fri 08.00-16.45 hrs; weekends and public holidays until 12.30 hrs.

Ceylon Tourist Board, P.O. Box 1504, 78 Steuart Place, Colombo 3. Tel: (1) 437 059. Fax: 437 953.

Aitken Spence Tours (representing Thomson Holidays), Lloyds Buildings, Sir Baron Mawatha, P.O. Box 5, Colombo.
Tel: 430892. Fax: 436382/422381.

British Embassy, 190 Galle Road, P.O. Box 1433, Colombo 3. Tel: 437336.

U.S. Embassy, 210 Galle Rd., P.O. Box 106, Colombo. Tel: 448007.

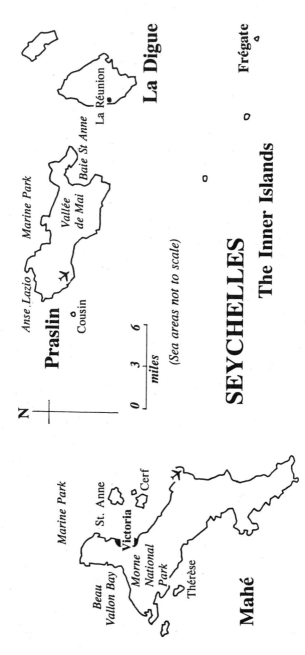

Praslin

Anse Lazio

Marine Park

Vallée de Mai

Baie St Anne

Cousin

La Digue

La Réunion

Frégate

N

0   3   6
miles

(Sea areas not to scale)

SEYCHELLES

The Inner Islands

Marine Park

St. Anne

Victoria

Cerf

Morne National Park

Beau Vallon Bay

Thérèse

Mahé

Chapter Eight

Seychelles

8.1 Jewel of the Indian Ocean

Around 115 Seychelles islands are sprinkled over 150,000 square miles of the Indian Ocean. Group the whole lot together, and the total area is a little larger than the Isle of Wight. If you want frenzied nightlife, the nearest is at least 1,000 miles away – in Mombasa on the Kenya coast, for instance.

Choose your island, and you can play out the Robinson Crusoe fantasy, exploring palm-shaded beaches with not a single footprint except your own. All you hear is birdsong, the gentle rustle of coconut trees, and the music of your Desert Island CDs if you haven't run out of batteries.

The tropical setting is perfect for sun-worship, water-sport and honeymoons. The climate is ideal, staying year-round in the 80's F. Annual rainfall is heavy, watering the luscious green scenery. But downpours are usually brief, freshening up the atmosphere, with the sun soon re-appearing.

There are two basic seasons on the Seychelles. November to April is warm and humid, the time of the northwest monsoon. May to October sees a small drop in temperature due to the cooler southeast monsoon. The islands are outside the cyclone belt, making extreme high winds rare.

These uninhabited islands were charted by the Portuguese in 1502 – though Arab traders may have called earlier – but the first recorded visit was by an English ship in 1609. The next visitors came in 1742, when the French took possession. They named the group Séchelles in honour of a Controller of Finances in the court of Louis XV.

Nothing much happened until 1768 when a settlement was established on Mahé. The main impetus came from a colonial official and botanist named Pierre Poivre, who neatly translates as Peter Pepper. He introduced spice plantations, in a bid to deprive the Dutch of their moneymaking monopoly of the spice trade. A major plus point for the Seychelles was the freedom from hurricanes.

To work the plantations, slaves were shipped in from Mauritius, followed by the introduction of freed slaves from East Africa. The plantation owners and supervisors were French. Later came Indian small traders and Chinese.

In 1814, the Treaty of Paris ceded the islands to Britain, who continued the French policy of administering them as a dependency of Mauritius. Later the Seychelles became a separate crown colony, but the French element lingered on, to produce today's official Creole language – a French patois mixed with Indian words, African and English. There is a parallel mixture of skin colours.

The plantation crops of coconuts, cinnamon and vanilla remain important, while a number of the Plantation Houses have been adapted to the new crop of tourism. Holidaymakers enjoy the spicy tropical blend of sunshine, natural beauty, creole cuisine and 20th-century island-hopping.

Pace-setters for the islands are elderly giant tortoises who rummage through thickets of cashew trees, eating the juicy fruit and leaving the nuts. Like the protected tortoises, nobody hassles you in the Seychelles.

The islands offer a range of interest; so it's worth visiting at least one other during your stay. Mostly they can be visited by boat, or by air to a few larger ones.

About half the islands are of volcanic origin, solidly built of granite with central peaks and narrow coastal strips.

The remaining islands are coral including the world's largest atoll, Aldabra – the furthest removed from the main group, 630 miles from Mahé. Most of the coral atolls (circular reefs that enclose a lagoon) are uninhabited.

8.2 Arrival & orientation

With a filled-out landing card, go through Immigration and Customs. Note: even if you pass through the Green Channel, officers often search luggage. Allowances are basically the same as for entering the UK, and it's well worth taking in your duty-free litre of spirits.

Through the doors, travel agency reps await their clients for a brief drive to Mahé hotels, or for connecting air links to other islands.

8.3 At your service

Money: The currency unit is the Seychelles Rupee (SRe singular, SRs plural), divided into 100 cents. Reckon around 7.50 Seychelles Rupees for £1 sterling, or five to the US dollar. Check current exchange rates from any local bank or newspaper.

Hotels exchange currency or travellers cheques, but banks give a slightly better rate. They are mainly in Victoria, but there are also some village banks. Most banks are open 8.30-13.30 Mon-Fri, and 8.30-11.00 hrs on Sat. Sterling everywhere is very easy to change.

Airport banks are open when international flights arrive. This is a good time to change currency, especially if you are continuing to another island.

American Express, Access/MasterCard and Visa are widely accepted, but Diners Club has more limited use.

Transport: Bus services on Mahé and Praslin are low cost, with fares between 2 and 5 rupees. Ask for times and destinations at your hotel reception. Services operate mainly from 5.30-21.30 hrs, but on Saturday afternoons the system closes down. Mahé's bus terminal is on Palm Street, Victoria.

Most comfort-lovers prefer taxi transport. Cabs await at Mahé's major hotels, the airport and at Victoria's two cab-ranks – on Albert Street, next to the craft centre; and facing the Post Office on Independence Avenue. Tariffs are set by the government but it's advisable to agree the price before setting off. Pre-booking a taxi is also a good idea.

Car hire: For complete independence, hire a car. On offer for about £46 a day are soft-topped Suzuki jeeps or open Mini-Mokes which should be driven with extreme caution. Regular saloons are safer. Rental can be arranged through your tour rep. Cars available for hire are very limited, so it's wise to book ahead.

The speed limit is 40 kph in built up areas and 65 kph elsewhere, with left-hand driving. Many roads are steep and winding, with ditches each side and no pavements, though highways on Mahé are well surfaced and maintained. Take special care on wet roads and behind heavy vehicles. The locals make little use of mirrors, so always toot before overtaking.

Petrol costs around £1 per litre. Keep your tank topped up. There are only six filling stations on Mahé, and all except the one at Victoria are closed weekends from Saturday noon.

8.4 Mahé and Praslin

Largest of the Seychelles islands is 60-sq-mile Mahé, home to 90% of the entire population. With its international airport, Mahé is also the economic and political centre of the Seychelles. The only town is Victoria, rated among the world's smaller capitals, with population of 25,000.

Victoria's principal attractions are a cathedral, a clock tower that's a replica of the clock outside London's Victoria Station, a colourful market, a small National Museum and the 15-acre Botanical Gardens which has a fine collection of orchids. Many colonial style houses are built of massive coral blocks that glisten like white marble.

From Victoria harbour the *Starfish* sub-aqua vessel operates around the five tiny islands of the Ste Anne Marine National Park for glass-bottom viewing or snorkelling, with time ashore at Round Island or Cerf.

Incidentally, 46% of the Seychelles landmass has been designated as National Parks, Reserves or Protected Areas.

The interior of Mahé abounds with lush coconut plantations, and mountains that rise to the 2993-ft.

peak of Morne Seychellois, west of Victoria. The steep passes make driving slow but afford breath-taking views of neighbouring islands.

The south of the island is very quiet and has beautiful deserted beaches with local villages untouched by the developments elsewhere on Mahé.

Huge granite cliffs have been sculpted by the winds and sea spray, and look more like monuments than natural wonders.

Mahé claims 68 golden beaches, though many are either very secluded, or – south of the airport – too shallow for swimming. The most popular beach is Beau Vallon Bay in the north, which features two miles of white sand and ample watersport facilities.

Two other top-grade beaches are the often deserted Grande Intendance down the west coast; and Grande Anse (French for cove) on the mid west coast.

Both these beaches have dramatic surf conditions. Take special care of the strong undertow. There are no lifeguards anywhere in the Seychelles.

Praslin

Measuring seven miles by five, Praslin is the second largest island in the Seychelles – 3 hours by boat or 15 minutes by air from Mahé. Beachside hotels are used on island-hopping circuits, or for complete holidays. Otherwise Praslin is the top choice for day trips from Mahé, often with La Digue included in the package.

A sightseeing highlight is the famous Vallée de Mai, the site of a prehistoric forest. In this valley grow the remarkable Coco-de-Mer palms which yield huge 40-pound double coconuts shaped like a woman's pelvis – rated as the largest seed in the vegetable kingdom.

It takes 25 years for the tree to bear fruit and several hundred years to reach full maturity. In this Garden of Eden live rare Black Parrots, Bulbuls and Fruit Pigeons.

Many longer-stay visitors hire a car to go bumping around, exploring the beaches. Among the most perfect is Anse Lazio on the north coast. Some beaches have a seasonal problem with seaweed.

8.5 Hopping to the smaller islands

Here's an island-hopping selection, readily accessible from Mahé or Praslin. Ask your tour rep to make arrangements for day excursions; or, planned in advance, ask your travel agent to book a stop-over package. Note that only ten kilos of luggage are allowed on inter-island flights, but you can leave excess baggage at your base hotel.

The most popular one-day trip from Mahé includes a range of transport: by air to Praslin, boat to La Digue and scenic sightseeing by ox-cart. That package costs about £105 including lunch.

Frégate: Located about 25 miles from Mahé, this one-square-mile island can be reached in 15 minutes by Air Seychelles. Flights land close to Plantation House which doubles as a hotel. Within its small area, Frégate offers five superb beaches with good potential for swimming and snorkelling. Rated as the most beautiful beach in the Seychelles, Anse Victorin was picked by *The Observer* newspaper in 1993 as "The Best Beach in the World."

La Digue: Only a 30-minute boat trip from Praslin, or three hours from Mahé, the island has no direct access by air except by helicopter from Mahé. Fourth largest in the Seychelles, La Digue is three miles by two of granite rock, surrounded by coral.

Here you can enjoy a serenity that has been little changed by the 20th century. Apart from a few cars, the island transport system relies on ox-wagons and bicycles. An ox-powered tour can take you to the most scenic parts of the island, where some traditional style houses are located. Some of the natural granite rock formations look as though carved by Henry Moore.

Food and refreshment are available at the idyllic La Digue Lodge on the west coast. On a day trip there's leisure time to enjoy the scenery or have a swim before taking the return boat to Praslin or Mahé. Like several other islands, La Digue has a good name for bird preservation – giving woodland sanctuary to 30 or more pairs of the rare black paradise flycatcher.

Bird Island: You have probably chosen the Seychelles for their beauty and idyllic seclusion – and possibly for what is arguably the most memorable experience of all: sunset over Bird Island.

From April to September, just as the sun has dipped, literally thousands of sea birds rise into the air, wheeling and plummetting with wings beating.

Only 30 minutes by air from Mahé, this island is the breeding ground for two million sooty terns who arrive in May and depart in October with their million young.

Besides these migrants, Bird Island is also frequented by fairy and noddy terns, cardinals, ground doves, mynahs, crested terns and plovers. A prime choice for bird lovers!

Bird Island has also made it into the Guinness Book of Records, thanks to Esmerelda, a giant tortoise who is 200 years old and weighs 305 kilos, making it the oldest and heaviest tortoise in the world. Despite the name, Esmerelda is male.

For around £132 you can spend a whole day and overnight on Bird Island, with all meals, accommodation and transport included.

Cousin: This 27-hectare island sanctuary is owned by BirdLife and administered by the International Council for Bird Preservation, which ensures a safe home for the rare Seychelles brush warbler.

Other species include the Seychelles fody, the turtle dove, fairy terns, noddies and bridled terns. This nature reserve for endangered species may be visited by a maximum of 20 people, only on Tuesdays, Thursdays and Fridays. The location is 1½ hours by boat from Praslin.

Desroches: This low-lying coral island is located 150 miles south of Mahé – a one-hour flight on Air Seychelles.

There's only one hotel, stretching along one of the finest beaches, with a working coconut plantation to explore.

The Lodge cultivates its own fruit and veg, and rears cattle, sheep, pigs and chickens.

Silhouette: The third largest island in the archipelago, Silhouette lies 12 miles from the northwest coast of Mahé, with access by helicopter. It has no roads – only paths through the equatorial forest. This walkers' paradise rears to the peak of 2600-ft Morne Daubin. Tobacco, coffee, cinnamon and avocados are grown.

8.6 All the water sports

The Seychelles offer some of the world's best conditions for tropical swimming, snorkelling and scuba diving. Personal protection against the sun is highly important. However, there are a few additional points to remember:

• Shell collecting in protected areas and spear fishing is forbidden.

• If you are unfamiliar with a beach, always take local advice on the swimming conditions. Idyllic blue waters can have deceptively strong currents, especially between May and October.

• Wear diving slippers or beach shoes as protection from sharp coral and sea urchins.

The best months for scuba diving and snorkelling are April-May and October-November, which are also low-season months. Because of the spearfishing ban over the past decade, fish on the inshore reefs seem almost tame.

An annual underwater Festival called SUBIO is held in late November.

For deep sea fishing – marlin, tuna, kingfish, sailfish – reckon £400 to £500 a day for boat charter, which could be shared by four passengers.

8.7 Shopping

Shops are open Mon-Fri 8.30-12.00 hrs and 13-16 hrs. The colourful open-air market in Victoria sells fish, fruit and vegetables. Also available are local spices such as vanilla, cinnamon, cardamon and cloves. The strong black island tea may provide another taste reminder of the Seychelles.

There's a duty-free store at Camion Hall on Albert Street, Victoria. Purchases are delivered to the airport, ready for your departure.

Don't buy articles made from turtle or tortoise shell, coral, or shark bone. All are protected by conservation laws, and their import is banned by most countries.

Instead, consider buying other products from the Craft Village on Mahé's east coast, 9 miles south of Victoria, where a museum displays many household items made from coconut. There's good choice of mother-of-pearl rings and pendants; boxes and walking sticks carved from local wood; or even polished Coco-de-Mer nuts.

8.8 Eating out

The Seychelles offer a wide choice of dishes. Local fresh fish, pork and chicken are cooked in a variety of different ways, blending local herbs and oriental spices. Besides Creole cooking, there's also choice of Chinese, French and Italian but no McDonald's.

Since the Seychelles islands are small and hilly, with limited land suitable for farming, many food items such as beef, apples, oranges and all dairy products must be imported. Hence restaurant meals tend to be expensive - £20 or more for a hotel buffet, or £13 for an average main course.

Local dishes and specialities are excellent and offer good value, especially the fresh fish. Try the excellent tuna steak and octopus curry. A pizza or a hamburger and chips will cost £6 or £7.

All wines and spirits are imported, and are costly. However, Seybrew – the local lager beer produced under German licence – is very good. Likewise Guinness is locally brewed, but is served chilled. Soft drinks are also produced under the Seybrew brand-name.

As a guide expect to pay about £3 for a glass of wine or £16 for a bottle; £2 to £3 for a beer; £3 to £6 for a short; 80p for a coffee.

Seychelles tea is of good quality and coffee is imported from East Africa; but the milk is usually evaporated, condensed or UHT. Mains water is chlorinated but may cause mild upsets in tummies that don't like the flavour. You'll have fewer problems with bottled water (costing £2.40), or the water usually provided in flasks in your hotel room.

8.9 Nightlife

The Seychelles are at least 1,000 miles away from sophisticated nightlife. Larger hotels may feature a disco, and occasional performances of local folk music, or traditional Sega dancing of the type seen in Mauritius. But that's about the wildest it gets.

A Sunset Cruise out of Victoria includes guitar music, romantic songs, sundowners, and an evening of traditional folk-dancing to go with a creole barbecue. Gamblers can try their luck in casinos at Beau Vallon Bay Hotel and at Plantation Club.

8.10 Quick facts

Total area: 171 sq miles, equal to 1¼ times the Isle of Wight; 2½ times size of Washington, DC.
Coastlines: 307 miles.
Time: GMT +4.
Natural resources: fish, coconut and cinnamon trees.
Land use: arable land 4%; permanent crops 18%; meadows and pastures 0%; forest and woodland 18%; other 60%.
Population: 70,000, growth rate 0.9%
Life expectancy: 66 years male, 75 years female.
Fertility rate: 2.5 children born per woman.
Ethnic groups: Seychellois – mixture of Asian, African and European.
Language: The official language is Creole, but English and French are widely spoken.
Religion: Catholic 90%; Anglican 8%.
Literacy: 58% – male 56%, female 60%.
Work force: 28,000; industry and commerce 31%, government 20%, services 21%; agriculture and fishing 12%.
Capital: Victoria, Mahé, population 25,000.
Independence: 29 June 1976 (from UK).
Government: now a multi-party democracy, after years of being one-party state.
Suffrage: universal at age 17.
Legal system: based on French civil law and English common law.
Executive branch: president, Council of Ministers.
Judicial branch: Court of Appeal, Supreme Court.

The economy: Dominated by tourism. To reduce over-reliance on this service industry, government encourages farming, fishing and light manufacture. Growth rate up to 7%.

Exports: fish, copra and cinnamon bark.

Farming: represents 7% of GDP, mostly subsistence apart from coconuts and cinnamon.

8.11 Hints and useful addresses

Electricity: 240 volts AC, 50 Hz. UK type square 3-pin plugs are commonly used in hotels. But it's still worth packing a travel adaptor for any electric gadgets you may wish to use.

A torch may be useful if staying overnight on the smaller islands.

What to pack: Daytime dress is very casual and informal. But all hotels request that gentlemen wear long trousers for evening dining. A lightweight raincoat or folding umbrella is advisable in case of sudden tropical downpours.

Laundry: Reckon average charges of £4 per shirt or £5 per dress. No dry cleaning available.

Tipping: Some hotel and restaurant tariffs include service charges. Otherwise 10% is normal practice.

Phone: Check the cost before phoning home! You can pay £10 for minimum 3 minutes, plus £3 for each further minute. Calls from hotels with operator assistance can often include a service charge.

The international dialling code for Seychelles is (010 from UK) +248 followed by the local 6-digit number (no area codes required).

Mail: Send your postcards early, as airmail can take up to a week to reach the UK. Post Offices are open 8-16 hrs Mon-Fri, and 8-12 Sat.

Security: There is some petty crime, but violence against tourists is rare. Keep valuables in hotel safes, and lock hotel windows at night. It is unwise for women to swim alone at isolated beaches.

Departure: Try to keep your luggage within 20 kilos, especially if you travel back via Kenya. Otherwise, excess baggage charges may be levied.

The airport operates a duty-free shop which is reasonably well stocked with drinks and perfumes. There is a café on both sides of customs and immigration.

Seychelles Tourist Office, 2nd Floor, Eros House, 111 Baker Street, London W1M 1FE.
Tel: (0171) 225 1670. Fax: (0171) 487 5756.
Open 9-16 hrs, Mon-Fri.
Seychelles High Commission – same address as above. Tel: (0171) 224 1660.
Seychelles Tourist Office, 820 Second Avenue, Suite 900 F, New York, NY 10017.
Tel: 212-687-9766. Fax: 212-922-9177.

Addresses in Seychelles
Seychelles Tourist Board, Independence House, P.O. Box 92, Victoria, Mahé. Tel: 225333.
National Travel Agency (representing Thomson Holidays), Kingsgate House, PO Box 611, Victoria, Mahé. Tel: 224900.
British High Commission, Victoria House, Victoria, Mahé. Tel: (248) 223055.
U.S. Embassy, 4th Floor, Victoria House, PO Box 251, Victoria, Mahé. Tel: (248) 225256.

Chapter Nine

Mauritius

9.1 Coral island paradise

Mauritius is a perfect destination for the lover of water-sports – sailing, snorkelling, fishing, scuba-diving, water-skiing, windsurfing. The tropical island offers safe coral viewing, in totally calm lagoon waters with no currents or sharks.

Soft sand, brilliant water, French cuisine and good service in the total comfort of beach-resort hotels: it makes a completely satisfying package for total relaxation. Many holidaymakers don't stir beyond the boundaries of their chosen beachside hotel, even if they're not on honeymoon. But Mauritius offers good sightseeing for anyone who rents a self-drive car or takes a guided tour.

Apart from the freeway that curls from the southeast corner of the island through Curepipe and Port Louis to the north, highways are narrow, used as a general social centre for goats, dogs and hens.

Most visitors are delighted with the cheerful friendliness of the locals. Whenever you get lost, smiling villagers give directions. African, Creole, Indian or Chinese – they are always eager to help!

Village names often reflect the ethnic character of a settlement. You can have a flat tyre fixed in Mecca, or take a wrong turning and end up in Yemen or Benares.

Local houses are a mixture of everything from shanties to elegant and well-painted villas. TV aerials sprout from unlikely-looking dwellings. Sari-clad women gossip at garden gates, or do the family washing at irrigation canals that pass through every village and alongside every road.

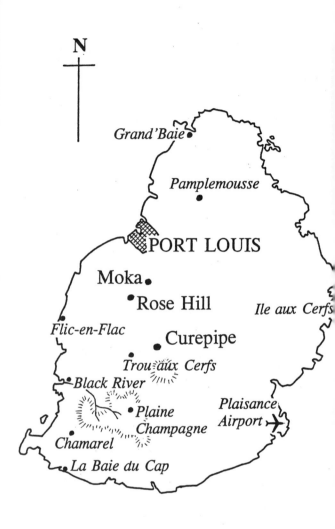

MAURITIUS

0   5   10
miles

Especially beautiful is the coastal scenery of the south. In La Baie du Cap, the fabulous coastline is superb. Anywhere on European shores, the location would be as famous as the Bay of Naples.

Every mile or two, another gorgeous tropical vista opens out: a golden beach, fringed with palms; a calm blue lagoon reaching to white breakers on the coral reef; mountains rearing up like fever charts to the sky; and green billiard cloths of sugar-cane that follow every contour of the coastal plain and mountain foot-hills.

Plan your meal-breaks and refreshment stops in advance! Along miles of scenic coastline or mountain panoramas, suitable tourist restaurants and bars are scanty. Best policy is to make meal and refreshment halts at the international beach hotels, spaced around each corner of the island.

Wherever you're based, anywhere in Mauritius can easily be visited on day trips. A typical leading hotel chain offers interchange facilities of room, meals and sports within the group, to ensure the widest possible range of sightseeing, leisure and entertainment.

From most hotels you can spend enthralling hours in a glass-bottom boat at the coral reef, where the marine world is as interest-packed as an African game reserve. Shoals of multi-coloured and striped tropical fish dart amid the fantastic growth of coral. With bright sunlight sparkling into the emerald waters, down to the yellow sand on the sea bottom, the coral gleams as though decorated with luminescent paint.

Only 400 years ago Mauritius was an uninhabited island, with the turkey-sized dodo flourishing as the principal occupant. Then Dutch explorers came, and passing mariners and pirates ate all the dodos until they were extinct by 1681. The French settled in 1721 and started sugar plantations, importing East African slaves to work them.

The English took over the island in 1810, and – with the later abolition of slavery – brought in Hindu Indian contract labourers. Moslem small traders followed; and the Chinese, who settled especially in Port Louis.

Hence the population today is composed of a melting-pot mixture of Europeans, Africans, Indians and Chinese. The dominant group is Indian, both Hindu and Moslem, totalling two-thirds of the island's population. It all makes a fascinating mosaic of race, religion, culture and language.

Around 300,000 Creoles – principally Roman Catholic – are the product of 200 years of interbreeding: African, with French or English blood, Indian or Chinese. There is every rainbow permutation of pinkish white to jet black; curly hair and straight; features that mingle Europe, Africa and Asia.

The local whites are mostly French, about 10,000; and some 1,000 British and other expatriates. The French still dominate the Mauritian economy – the sugar barons, and those who diversified into other industries and professions, including tourism and hotel business. The French colonial style sets the tone for upper-crust social life.

In the principal hotels, the cuisine is basically French, but with English style breakfasts. Certainly a question of getting the best of both worlds!

Best of all is the climate. Mauritius enjoys steady maximum temperatures that vary only between 77° F in June and 86° in February. January to April sees the heaviest rainfall, which comes usually in short downpours followed by sun and blue skies. The cyclonic months are November to March.

The winter season of May-September is drier, in the high 70's. The southeast trade winds bring more rain and somewhat cooler evenings to the southern and eastern sides of the island, compared to the north and west. Year-round there is a daily average of 7 hours' sunshine.

9.2 Arrival & orientation

Seen from the air, a white necklace encircles the island, marking the breakers on the coral reef. There is blue Indian ocean on the outside, then an emerald green lagoon, and a fringe of golden beach. An occasional gap in the reef permits passage of small boats. The grid pattern of enormous sugar plantations reaches to the mountain slopes.

On disembarkation, you should complete an immigration card to correspond with the dates shown on your return ticket. Then pass through health control where details of your passport and hotel are noted. Collect your luggage and go through Customs.

Beyond a set of doors, tour representatives await their clients. For Thomson guests, reps of the local agency, White Sand Tours, wear a green uniform.

Plaisance Airport in the southeast is linked to Port Louis and the northern resorts by a freeway. The beautiful drive to your beach hotel will introduce you to the lush green fertility of this mountainous island of volcanic origin. Villages are spread around the narrow coastal plains, with a high plateau in the interior.

Fifty short fast-flowing rivers feed the irrigation system. The mountaintop catchment area gets a torrential annual rainfall of close on 200 inches. At Curepipe, which seems almost perpetually veiled in mist and cloud, rainfall is much less. On the southwest coast it is barely 25 to 30 inches.

Hence the need for irrigation, especially on the west coast. Road signs warn of "overhead irrigation". Great fountains of water are pumped over the sugar-cane fields and onto passing motorists, cyclists and pedestrians. Catch the sun right, and you get a colour picture effect of a moving rainbow over the cane fields, with a black mountain peak looming above.

9.3 At your service

Money: The Mauritian Rupee (Rs) is divided into 100 cents (cs). Visitors may import Mauritius notes up to a value of Rs 700 and take out Rs 350. The exchange rate has been around 28 Mauritian Rupees to the pound, but check current rates on arrival.

Banks are generally open 10-14 hrs Mon-Fri, and 9.30-11.30 on Saturday. Travellers cheques and cash can be changed at your hotel, but usually at a less favourable rate.

Visa, Access/MasterCard, Amex and Diners are acceptable credit cards.

Transport: virtually every corner of the island is accessible by the local bus services, which are slow but cheap. Most visitors prefer to use taxis or self-drive car.

Taxis are distinguished by their white registration plates with black numbers (the reverse from private cars). It's always advisable to agree the fare before starting a journey, though meters are being introduced. Standard prices are set by the tourist board, and can be checked with your hotel or rep. The tariffs include the return mileage, so it's often cheaper for the driver to wait and bring you back, subject to payment for waiting time.

Car hire is readily available for drivers of minimum age 23, with a clean driving licence which is at least one year old. International companies such as Avis, Hertz, Europcar etc charge about £45 per day for a mini-moke or £55 for a car.

The scenic delights of Mauritius, with its villages, hills and beaches, make superb sightseeing. Buy a good map, as minor roads are often poorly signposted, making it easy to get lost. Driving is on the left. Night driving is not recommended.

9.4 Places to visit

If you prefer to be guided rather than self-driving around the island there are well-organised excursions available, some with boat trips included. Just to whet your appetite, here are brief details of places to visit.

Port Louis is the colourful capital, based on the sheltered harbour founded by the French in 1736. Many of the principal buildings are in French colonial style, especially around the main square called Place d'Armes.

There's an 18th-century Government House (with Queen Victoria's statue in front), a Municipal Theatre, some French-built barracks and a Natural History Museum.

The most colourful area is the covered market, vibrant with the ethnic mixture. Equally colourful is the neighbouring Chinatown sector, where most of the island's Chinese are tightly grouped.

The original French parade ground called Champ de Mars was converted into a race-course in 1812. The Mauritius Turf Club is claimed as the second oldest turf club in the world.

Curepipe is well placed on the island's central plateau, with good shops and restaurants. It's the main residential centre.

Trou aux Cerfs, near Curepipe, is a spectacular extinct volcano which offers magnificent island views from the rim.

Plaine Champagne to the south is the highest point of Mauritius (2428 ft), with superb views of the heavily forested **Black River Gorges**.

This indigenous forest is one of the few areas that survived clearance for sugar and tea plantations. Natural and artificial lakes preserve the wilderness intact.

On the forest edges are tangled masses of wild raspberries, and a glut of guavas. Switch off the car engine, and there's nothing but total silence, except for bird song and the beat of butterfly wings.

Chamarel, reached down a winding road, is a beautiful location of vari-coloured dunes of red, blue, yellow and purple earth with a neighbouring waterfall.

Casela Bird Park, near Flic-en-Flac beach on the west coast, is a 20-acre setting for a worldwide collection of birds, including the very rare Mauritian pink pigeon. Alas, no dodo!

Grand'Baie is the tourist focal point of the northern coast and its popular beaches, and is the main centre for yachting and other water sports.

Ile Aux Cerfs is the ultimate island paradise just off the east coast. Concentrate on sun, sea and watersports without worrying about where the next iced cocktail is coming from. Celebrate with a seafood barbecue.

Pamplemousses Botanical Gardens were founded by the French botanist Pierre Poivre in 1767 on a 60-acre site, where he introduced spices from the Dutch Indies.

9.5 All the water sports

The translucent emerald green waters of bays and lagoons are sheer paradise for all the standard water sports. Some hotels offer free windsurfing, snorkelling and sailing, with instruction if required.

Scuba diving costs around £21 for one dive, or £175 for ten. Divers must provide proof of experience – log book, for example. But of course lessons are available for beginners.

A few optimistic scuba divers still go looking for sunken pirate treasure. Several pirate treasure maps are in existence, but the details are usually a bit vague. Far more rewarding is to explore the coral reefs, goggling at the tropical fish, darting amid their coral garden of pink, green, mauve and blue.

Beyond the reef, Mauritian waters abound with big game fish. Try and catch a tuna, bonito, or even a marlin. The world Marlin Championships are held at La Pirogue, where several records have been established. Best fishing grounds are off the north-west and south-west coasts, where well equipped boats operate. Your tour rep can make reservations for day fishing and special overnight charters.

Among the land sports, 9-hole golf is available at St Geran for approx £35 (free for St Geran guests), with club hire at £9. Green fees at Trou aux Biches, on the north west coast, likewise cost £35, with club hire costing around £6 with no charge for trolley hire. At Belle Mare Plage, golf on the 18-hole course is free for guests, club hire £9.

Horse riding is available at about £16 an hour.

9.6 Shopping

The widest range of shopping is in Port Louis, Rose Hill and Curepipe. Local souvenirs such as baskets, holdalls, woodwork, hand-embroidered table cloths, table mats, blouses and saris, tortoise shell and horn work are among the best buys.

Indian jewellery and pottery, macramé work, Chinese embroidery, knitwear and necklaces are available in all the main souvenir shops and at the beach hotels.

The local Green Island rum, costing around £3 a bottle, is also worth taking home as part of your duty-free allowance.

9.7 Eating out

The most pleasant surprise about Mauritius is the excellent cuisine, with choice of French, Indian, Chinese and Creole. Quite modest restaurants feature all four cuisines. A typical small establishment can offer menu choice of lobster cooked in ten different styles, ten styles for crab and eight for prawn. Sea-food is excellent, and there is an exotic range of vegetables and tropical fruits.

Fortunately for today's visitors, the French occupied Mauritius for 95 years and set culinary standards. Even though French tenure ended in 1810, the cuisine lives on. Those standards are maintained through the sheer numbers of French visitors who come either direct from France, or from the neighbouring island of Réunion which is an overseas department of France.

Although you can choose French peppered steaks or English roast beef, it's worth sampling some of the indigenous cuisine.

There is varied and exotic choice of Indian and Creole curries, Muslim biryani's and a host of Chinese delicacies. In fact, a specialised text book has been written to include six hundred recipes of local cuisine.

Worth trying is the Creole cooking: very spiced, of African origin. Typical is the traditional Creole dish of boiled rice with meat or fish curry cooked with turmeric, aniseed, a pot-pourri of spices, oil and onions and served with diced tomatoes, red-hot pimentos and pickled mango.

Also available is a full range of wines, spirits and tropical cocktails. Quench your thirst with coconut milk laced with the excellent Mauritian white rum. The local Mauritian beer has won international awards.

9.8 Nightlife

In the leading hotels, a band or disco plays every night. Generally, evening entertainment is fairly low-key, with in-house cabaret or film shows.

Special to Mauritius is a *Sega* evening, normally held once or twice a week. This indigenous music, song and dance is African in origin, dating from the days of slavery, 200 years ago.

In its primitive, highly erotic form, these earthy folk dances are held at weekends around camp fires in the shanty communities, with rum to fuel the dancers' enthusiasm. In its more cultivated, luxury hotel version, the Sega soon becomes popular with visitors, once they have learned the basic shuffle with a rhythmic movement of the hips.

Several resort hotels offer casino gambling, with choice of roulette with a single zero, blackjack, poker, chemin de fer and slot machines. The croupiers and dealers are mostly good looking girls of all the Mauritian colours. The principal gaming rooms are at the Casino de Maurice in Curepipe.

9.9 Quick facts

Total area: 726 sq. miles, including Rodrigues and other smaller islands. About the size of Berkshire; or ten times the size of Washington, DC.
Coastline: 110 miles, ringed by coral.
Natural resources: arable land, fish.
Land use: arable land 54%; permanent crops 4%; meadows and pastures 4%; forest and woodland 31%; other 7%.
Population: 1,116,000, growth rate 0.8%
Life expectancy: 66 years male, 74 years female.
Fertility rate: 2.0 children born per woman.
Ethnic groups: Indo-Mauritian 68%, Creole 27%, Chinese 3%, Franco-Mauritian 2%.
Religion: Hindu 52%, Christian (mainly Catholic) 28%, Muslim 17%.
Literacy: 90%. Education free to university level.
Work force: 335,000; government services 29%; agriculture and fishing 27%; manufacturing 22%.
Capital: Port Louis. Population about 150,000.
Independence: 12 March 1968 (from UK).

Government: an independent parliamentary republic within the British Commonwealth.

Legal system: based on French civil law, with some elements of English common law.

Judicial branch: Supreme Court.

Political parties: Militant Socialist Movement (MSM), Mauritian Militant Movement (MMM), Mauritian Labour Party (MLP), Socialist Workers Front, Mauritian Social Democrat Party.

Suffrage: universal at age 18.

The economy: Dominated by sugar, occupying 90% of the cultivated land. With a stable government and expanding economy, Mauritius has diversified into tea and food crops, offshore banking, and light manufacture especially of textiles.

There has been dramatic real economic growth of 6.7% annually for the past decade, with negligible unemployment.

9.10 Festivals and public holidays

There are six public holidays with fixed dates: New Year Jan 1 & 2; Independence Day March 12; Labour Day May 1; All Saints Day Nov 1; and Christmas Day.

Another seven holidays are religious festivals with floating dates.

Chinese New Year comes in Jan/Feb, coloured red for happiness and with much use of crackers to ward off evil spirits.

Cavadee, also in the Jan/Feb period, is celebrated with Hindu fire-walking and sword-climbing ceremonies.

Maha Shivaratree is another Hindu festival in February, based on rituals from the Holy Ganges.

Holi is the time to stay close to your hotel if you don't like being deluged in coloured water.

Id-El-Fitr marks the end of Ramadan, the Muslim month of fasting.

Father Laval was a Catholic saint, credited with miraculous healing powers. In September pilgrims flock to his shrine in Port Louis.

Divali is a cheerful Hindu holiday celebrated in Oct/Nov, when flickering oil lamps in front of every home mark the victory of Rama over Ravana.

9.11 Hints and useful addresses

Electricity: 220/240 volts AC, 50 Hz. UK type 3-pin plugs are commonly used in hotels.

Airport tax of Rs 100 is levied on departure (but included in the tour price for Thomson clients).

Phone: The International dialling code for Mauritius is (010 from UK) +230 followed by the local 7-digit number (no area codes required).

Mauritius Government Tourist Office, 32 Elvaston Place, London SW7 5NW.
Tel: (0171) 584 3666. Fax: (0171) 225 1135.
Opening hours: Mon-Fri 9.30-13.00 & 14-17 hrs, closing 16.30 hrs on Fri.
Mauritius High Commission at same address.
Tel: (0171) 581 0294.
Mauritius Tourist Information Service, Port Executive Bldg, 8 Haven Ave, Port Washington, New York 11050.
Tel: (516) 944 3763; Fax: (516) 944 8453.
Embassy of Mauritius, Suite 441, 4301 Connecticut Ave., N.W., Washington, D.C. 20008. Tel: (202) 244-1491/2. Consulates in Los Angeles; tel: (818) 788-3720; and Atlanta, (404) 892-8733.

Addresses in Mauritius:
Mauritius Government Tourist Office, Emmanuel Anquetil Building, Sir S. Ramgoolam Street, Port Louis. Tel: 201 1703. Fax: 212 5142.
British High Commission, Lescasades Building, Edith Cavell Street, Port Louis.
Tel: 211 1365, or 211 1361.
U.S. Embassy, Rogers House, 4th Floor, John F. Kennedy St, Port Louis. Tel: (230) 208 9764/9. Fax: (230) 208 9534.